Executive summary

I0473760

Performance Management 2012

Performance Management as a discipline is at a crossroads in 2012. The reinvigoration of Performance Measurement started in the 1990s and it continued with an increase in the use of performance management systems. It is still a lot less mature compared to Project Management, Process Management and even Enterprise Architecture and this affects its relevance and credibility in the business environment. While improvements have been made in specific fields of knowledge, such as performance measurement and strategy implementation, the integration between organizational, operational and employee performance is not sufficiently addressed, neither in theory nor in practice. The lack of standards and of an integrated body of knowledge leaves room for interpretation and confusion.

In recent times, two messages with the potential of becoming catalysts of change were sent out by the economic environment. The financial crisis highlighted that the archaic command-and-control management structures may become dangerous in today's interconnected business environment. The second message comes from start-up technology companies, many employing fresh approaches to culture and management systems, with impressive results. Such messages send a strong signal that Performance Management needs to progress to a new phase of maturity. However, as it happens many times in life, in order to change, it is important to know yourself in the context of your operating environment.

Performance Management in 2012 is the first from a series of annual publications in which The KPI Institute will provide an overview of the state of the discipline. The current volume was developed through a qualitative research study, reviewing both primary collected data and secondary sources. It covers a variety of topics, from expert perspectives on the matter to keyword trends and review of governmental efforts in promoting Performance Management at national level.

There were three main editorial rules followed in the development of the content. At The KPI Institute, we believe that the knowledge base of each discipline is expanded by the combined efforts of practitioners, academic researchers and consultants. This triangulation of views represents a blueprint of the series. Secondly, opinions from experts based in Anglo-Saxon countries were balanced by opinions from all corners of the world, from El Salvador to UAE and from China to Algeria. Globalization should be considered not only in economic terms, but also in terms of knowledge and insight generation and sharing. Thirdly, the aim of the content was to be practical, so as to ensure relevance to the widest array of stakeholders. Moreover, the content balances insights from subject matter experts with specific details about events, resources and keyword trends.

Performance Management in 2012 also initiates the challenging thought that the future of this discipline is now in the hands of a new generation of professionals, ready for change and for a more integrated approach in terms of both the body of knowledge and the cooperation needed for its progression. It builds a strong foundation for restructuring the position of Performance Management as the main organizational capability which acts as the central nervous system, linking all other management systems and disciplines.

Work has already begun on launching additional publications in this series, in the second half of 2012. Feedback regarding this edition and input for future editions are highly appreciated by our team of researchers and should be directed at editor@kpiinstitute.org.

Editorial coordination:
Aurel Brudan

ID number: TKI0121001
ISBN: 978-1478181019

An appropriate citation for this report is:
The KPI Institute, 2012, Performance Management in 2012, Melbourne, Australia

Published by:
The KPI Institute
Life.lab Building
198 Harbour Esplanade, Suite 606
Melbourne Docklands, VIC 3008, Australia
Telephone (international):
+61 3 9670 2979
E-mail: office@kpiinstitute.org
www.kpiinstitute.org

Editorial coordination
Aurel Brudan

Editorial team
Jamil Diu, Johnson Kee, Andreea Muntean, Alexander Schwab, Lynn L. Wang, Han Zhang, Charlotte Xuan Zheng, Huijing Zhuang

Design
Valeriu Pernes, Xaba Pete

Introduction

Perspectives

Around the world

Trends

About the Report 04

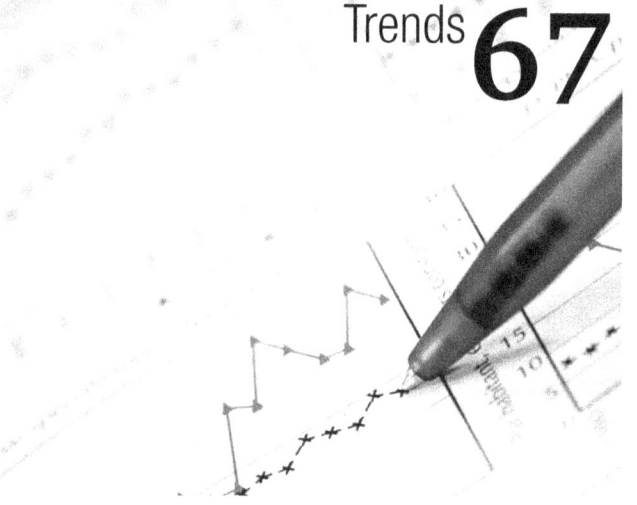

Trends 67

Around the World 45

Perspectives 06

Education **75**

Career
81

Resources **84**

Software **100**

About the report

Primary Sources

The development of *Performance Management in 2012* is the result of a qualitative research study conducted in February 2012, by The KPI Institute. Both primary and secondary research sources were used as part of the study.

Interviews

A total of 12 semi-structured interviews with academics, practitioners and consultants were conducted via telephone and email in February 2012, the data being processed in the subsequent weeks. They generated rich insights into the state of Performance Management as a discipline.

Legislation

Google Search was the source used to research legislation related to Performance Management in different countries. The data was collected based on searches using keywords including but not limited to the respective country's name, "Performance Management" and "legislation".

Trends in search

Thirty keywords that addressed Performance Management at individual, operational and organizational levels were searched and examined using Google AdWords and Google Trends. These tools were selected for their reputation of providing global search data, through trend graphs. Global Monthly Searches from Google AdWords were used to provide an overview of the popularity of these keywords through the use of the 12-month average of user queries for each respective keyword. Graphs from Google Trends were used to illustrate the change and volatility of each keyword's popularity.

Media exposure

Google News was the main data source, on levels of media exposure of Performance Management keywords. Ten keywords relating to Performance Management were used to search for levels of media exposure between 2000 and 2011. The search was restricted to these years as a significant amount of data was only available after year 2000.

THE KPI INSTITUTE PERFORMANCE MANAGEMENT RESEARCH

CURRENT RESEARCH PROGRAMS	TOPIC
PURPOSEFULIDENTITY.COM	MISSION, VALUES, VALUE DRIVERS, VISION STATEMENTS
INTEGRATINGPERFORMANCE.COM	INTEGRATED PERFORMANCE MANAGEMENT
BALANCEDSCORECARDREVIEW.COM	BALANCED SCORECARD
SMARTKPIS.COM	KEY PERFORMANCE INDICATORS

INTERESTED IN RESEARCH?

CONTACT US AT RESEARCH@KPIINSTITUTE.ORG FOR EXPLORING THE OPPORTUNITY TO ESTABLISH JOINT RESEARCH PROGRAMS

WHAT WE OFFER?

- FACILITATE ACCESS TO THE INSIGHTS OF OVER 50,000 PROFESSIONALS WITH AN INTEREST IN PERFORMANCE MANAGEMENT
- SUPPORT IN RESEARCH DESIGN, DATA ANALYSIS AND PUBLICATION
- ACCESS TO DISSEMINATION PLATFORMS

Education

Keywords relevant to Performance Management degrees and subjects were entered into Google search in order to discover universities which offered degrees or courses focusing on this area. International business schools rankings published by the Shanghai Jiaotong University were used as reference.

Conferences

The initial selection of Performance Management events was based on recommendations from experts who had either attended or were aware of such events. In addition, a list of renowned organizations or associations specialising in Performance Management were analysed and the events they organized were recorded.

Books

Searches were conducted on "Bestselling Books" and "Latest Published Books", based on 10 different keywords. The information was solely sourced from Amazon, which offers relatively objective and reliable information on book sales.

Articles

The most recently published articles in the field of Performance Management were found via "Latest Published Articles" search feature on the University of Melbourne Library Online Source and Google Scholar. Each potential source was then checked to determine whether the content of the article was relevant to Performance Management.

Portals

The initial selection of portals was based on recommendations from Performance Management experts and lists of useful portals that were available online. Web traffic statistics from Alexa and Compete were used to obtain the traffic ranking of selected websites.

Communities

The keyword "Performance Management" was searched in LinkedIn Groups in order to find the top 20 groups focused on Performance Management. Other keywords, such as "KPI" and "Balanced Scorecard" were also used to identify LinkedIn groups dedicated to these researched topics. Results (with the omission of software based groups) were then grouped into five categories, with the omission of software-based groups.

Job trends

The most popular job sites across six continents and two major markets (China and the Middle East) were used to assess for the number of positions available in the area of Performance Management. Furthermore, LinkedIn was used in order to increase the comprehensiveness of the search. The relative proportions of available jobs were then calculated for each respective region.

Salary

The Glassdoor website (http://www.glassdoor.com) was used to research information pertaining to the range of job salaries for both Strategy Managers and Performance Managers. The salary ranges across different industries are reported.

Software

Information pertaining to the trends in Performance Management software was derived and compiled from research reports published in 2011 and 2012 by Gartner.

Visual Summary

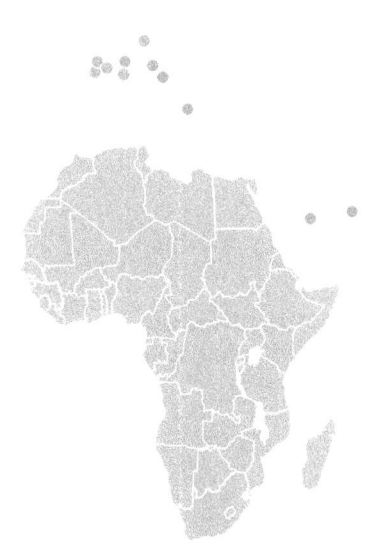

74% of Performance Management jobs
22% of all performance manager jobs, 28% of all strategy manager jobs
32% of strategy manager jobs

Institutions offering degrees in PM   (9)
Main events around PM in 2012   (14)

Map Overview

"Practice in this area is guided by judgment and intuition, rather than by hard scientific findings."

Prof. Kenneth Merchant
University of Southern California
USA

"We have to create metrics that achieve results without compromising the fairness of what we do."

Jodi Traversaro
State of California
USA

"Performance best practice = vision and strategy communication"

Enrique Rojo Granados
Insightforce Strategy Management Consultants
Mexico

"Performance Management should be more aware of initiatives and results aligned to strategy, rather than to operational results."

Isela Hernandez
Cinepolis Corporativo
Mexico

"The biggest barrier in implementing a good Performance Management program is the lack of understanding from management that having a good organizational governance system is a pre-requisite to start the Performance Management program."

Humberto E Della Torre
Grupo Calleja
El Salvador

"You need to work on several things: develop philosophy, develop concepts, develop theory, develop mythologies and develop technology, in order to have the adequate tools for performance monitoring and process modeling of any kind of organizations."

Ricardo Rodriguez-Ulloa
CENTRUM Católica
Peru

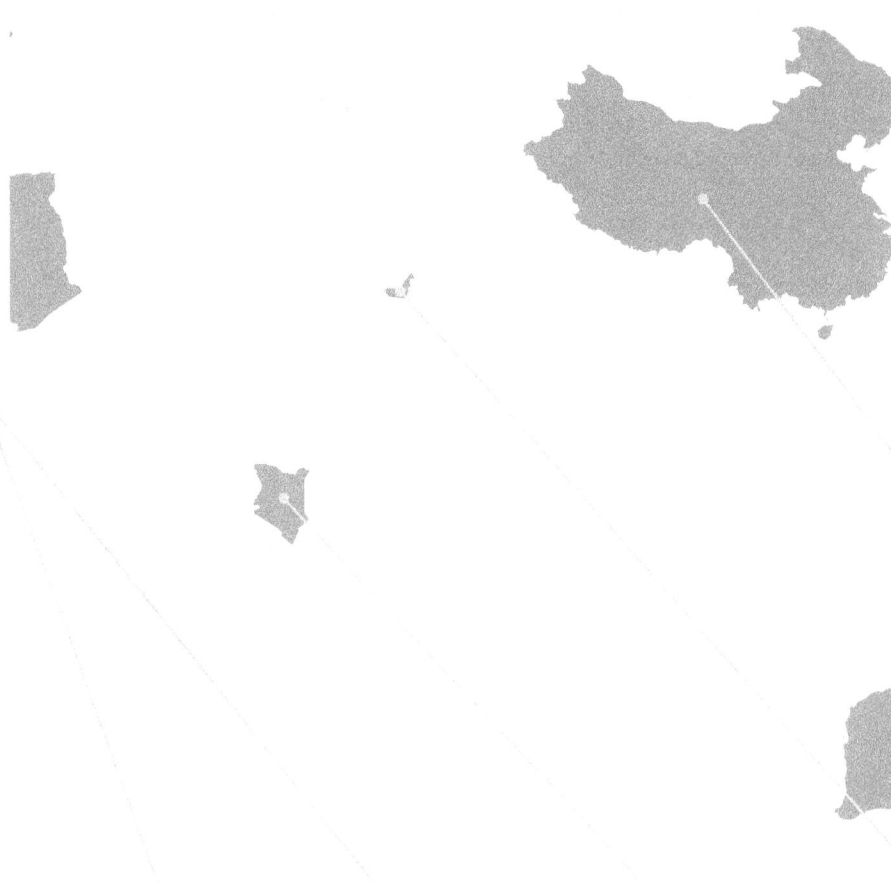

"Evaluating performance from a broader perspective is a key trend."

Sujay Nair
University of Melbourne
Australia

"I see the next big opportunity for research in the Performance Management field as focusing on ways to improve the way organizations are managed, rather than on improving how their work gets done, either internally and/or across end-to-end supply chains."

"If your system doesn't tell employees what to do, they won't understand the objectives and be able to link it back to the overall strategy. "

"Linking of the dots between strategic performance and individual performance is a key trend."

"Conflicts between local culture and Performance Management is a challenge."

"The proficiency in applying Performance Management is a challenge."

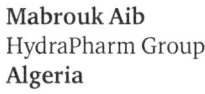

Alan Meekings	**Mabrouk Aib**	**Peter Ndaa**	**Ahmed Samy**	**Fengcai Qiu**
Landmark Consulting	HydraPharm Group	Balanced Scorecard	Western Region	Singapore Empower
UK	**Algeria**	Eastern Africa	Municipality	Consulting Group Pte. Ltd.
		Kenya	**UAE**	**China**

Introduction

13 questions - 12 interviews - academics . practitioners . consultants
Australia . China . El Salvador . Kenya . Mexico . Peru . UAE . UK . USA

Disciplines of human knowledge progress though the collective efforts of academics, consultants and practitioners. The following 12 interviews reveal insights on theory and practice, as well as emerging trends in Performance Management.

The same set of questions was put forward to each of the three types of professions. Question 13 varied depending on the type of professional.

1 What does the term Performance Management mean to you?

2 What drives interest in Performance Management?

3 What are your thoughts on the relationship between Performance Management at organizational, departmental and individual level?

4 What are the 2012 key trends in Performance Management from the perspective of your knowledge and experience in this field?

5 What aspects of Performance Management should be explored more through research?

6 Please provide some examples of organizations which you would recommend for study due to their approach to Performance Management and achievements.

7 Which are the main challenges of Performance Management in practice today?

8 What do you think should be improved in the use of Performance Management tools and processes?

9 What would you consider best practice in Performance Management?

10 Which aspects of Performance Management should be emphasized during educational programs?

11 What are the barriers in achieving higher levels of proficiency in Performance Management among practitioners?

12 What Performance Management question would you like to have answered?

13a We are developing a database of Performance Management subjects and degrees in Performance Management. What are your suggestions relevant to the database (i.e. subjects or degrees such as the Masters in Managing Organizational Performance)?

13b Which were the recent achievements in generating value from Performance Management in your organization?

13c As a consultant, what are the most common issues that your customers raised related to Performance Management? ■

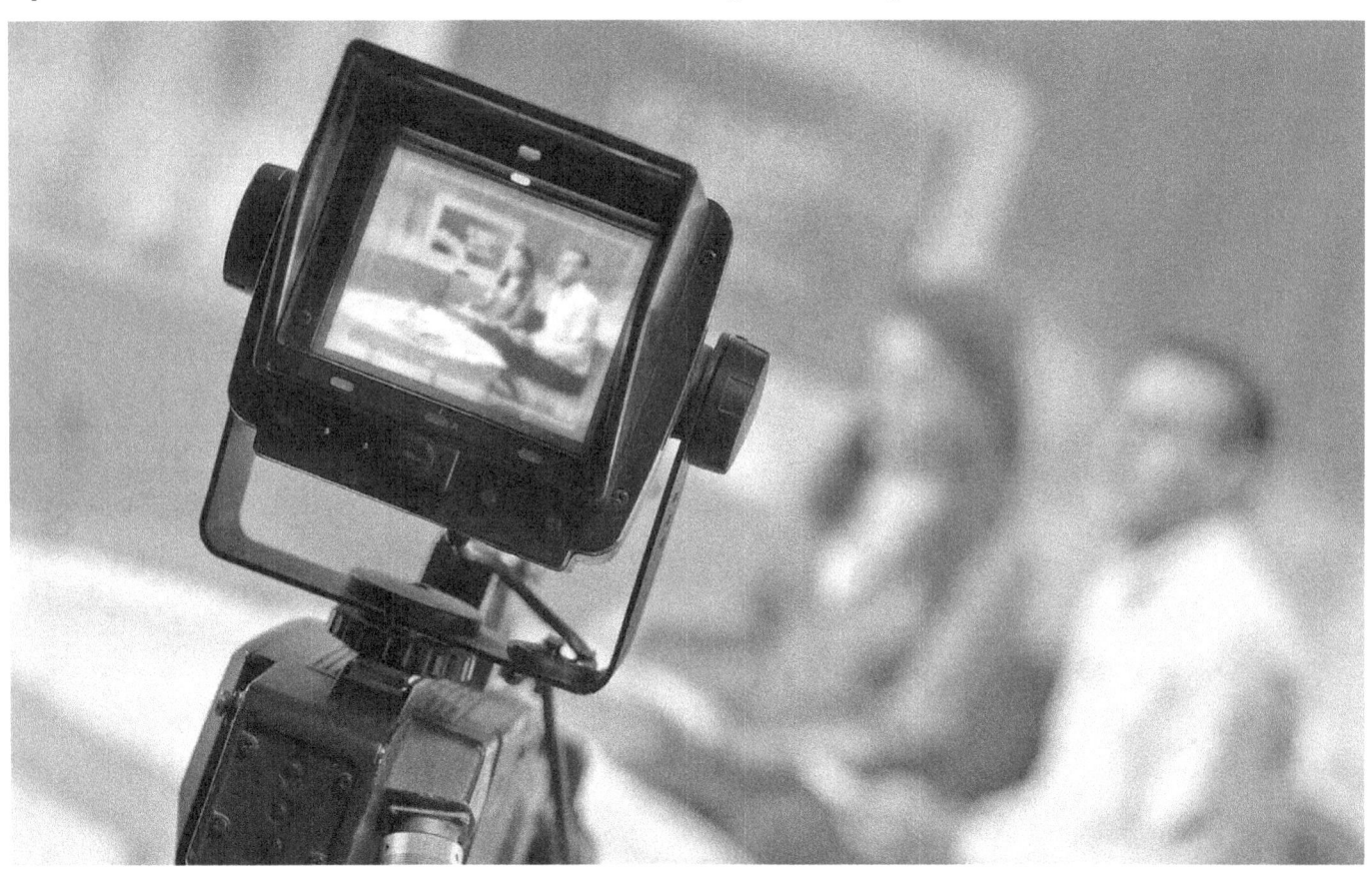

Global Perspectives

1 What does the term Performance Management mean to you?

Performance Management is a very broad term and as a result, different groups understand the concept in different ways. Anecdotal evidence reveals that most people perceive Performance Management as referring to individual Performance Management.

Performance Management is considered to be a series of management tools and processes used for connecting the individual, group and organizational levels of an organization. These processes monitor, control and manage the strategic and operational direction of an organization. Specifically, key practices may include setting priorities and operational plans, establishing targets and relevant KPIs. The goal of Performance Management processes is to help organizations achieve their desired results, oftentimes expressed through strategic objectives.

However, Performance Management is more than just about achieving strategic objectives. It also aims to drive continuous organizational improvement through constant reviewing and taking corrective actions, whilst continuing to make necessary adjustments to the Performance Management system.

2 What drives interest in Performance Management?

The popularity of Performance Management has grown at a rapid rate and has become part of organizations' core business processes. Furthermore, as organizations mature, the need for Performance Management systems shift from "preferable" to "must have". In contrast, in countries such as China, the public is not that interested in Performance Management and is in fact quite critical of it. Nevertheless, three main reasons were seen to drive interest in Performance Management.

1. Links with driving organizational objectives

The strong link between effective Performance Management systems and an organization's ability to successfully achieve its strategic objectives has been a main driving force behind the interest in Performance Management. In other words, there is a consensus that Performance Management can translate efforts into results via more efficient and effective operations.

2. Allows for organizational improvement

As effective Performance Management can help foster product and service innovation, excellent customer service, operational efficiency and productivity, Performance Management can act as

It is through the mandatory introduction of China Mobile's KPIs that that China Mobile has been able to have such success.

a driver for continuous improvement. Furthermore, Performance Management aids in the ongoing need to keep up with changes and levels of competition within different industry sectors.

3. Specific areas within Performance Management

Although the concept of Performance Management is popular, certain topics such as Balanced Scorecards have immensely driven general interest in Performance Management. The popularity of Balanced Scorecards has seen more Performance Management systems being implemented, however a major problem has been the fact that these systems have not been tailored to the specific needs (structure and culture) of organizations.

3 What are your thoughts on the relationship between Performance Management at organizational, departmental and individual level?

In theory, high performing individuals should lead to a high performing department which ultimately leads to a high performing organization. Generally it is agreed that alignment between the individual, departmental and organizational levels is necessary in order to achieve organizational success. However, in reality, most organizations do not have such well aligned Performance Management measures between the different levels, therefore much efficiency and effectiveness is lost. This can be attributed to leakages such as the objectives being poorly aligned or the lack of leadership capabilities.

Given the complexity of organizations today, it means that when designing a Performance Management system, it is impossible to say whether the individual or the organization level should have priority. This is because traditionally, individuals act in the interests of the department, which serves the organization. Organizations are more receptive to suggestions put forward at the departmental level and also the individual level. Effectively, there the relationship needs to be symbiotic.

4 What are the 2012 key trends in Performance Management from the perspective of your knowledge and experience in this field?

The growing popularity of Performance Management has meant organizations have begun to pay more attention to the trends in Performance Management. Although new trends are constantly appearing, below are three key trends in Performance Management for 2012.

1. Focus on soft Performance Management indicators

In the past, organizations have focused mainly on hard indicators (financial, productivity, production and market share measures); however, recently there has been much progress in understanding which non-financial measures of performance have an impact on financial performance.

This broadened view of performance measurement has meant that organizations and academics are looking beyond the shareholders' perspective. For example, there have been developments in indicators which measure organizational culture, power distribution, the environment, the political climate, social responsibilities and other cultural factors.

2. Strategic alignment

An integrated approach to Performance Management enables the "linking of dots" between strategic performance and individual performance. Whilst it is easy to create KPIs and Performance Management systems, it is crucial that Performance Management is integrated in the process of developing strategies in order to help focus efforts and measure the expected results.

3. Other trends

Other Performance Management trends in 2012 include the automation of Performance Management systems, increased transparency and collaboration. Other trends include Performance Management from a technological point of view and performance planning and culture.

5 What aspects of Performance Management should be explored more through research?

Some of the ideas proposed by the panel of 12 Performance Management practitioners, academics and consultants for being researched in more details are:

- How to create a combination-of-KPIs system. Financial KPIs, by themselves, are insufficient; we need to have soft non-financial KPIs which complement the overall Performance Management picture. Furthermore, how would these new KPIs be appropriately weighted in importance?
- Whether current Performance Management systems fit or need to be modified for the new generation that has recently joined the workforce, Generation Y.
- How to get people to adopt Performance Management in management practices. In other words, researching more about the link between Performance Management and the culture of the organizations. In particular, how to build the culture that accepts measurements and is adaptable to changing them.
- How to teach people about the benefits. Potential avenues could include more research into success stories in both the private and public sector.
- The integration of Risk Management with Performance Management with Strategic Management and combining them all into one framework.

6 Please provide some examples of organizations which you would recommend for study due to their approach to Performance Management and achievements.

Large organizations that are generally recognised to be well run or considered on "Best Company" lists are worth studying. Companies that have performed well include Google and Facebook. In addition, one can look at companies that have managed to sustain high levels of performance such as IBM, GE and Siemens A.G. These companies generally have best practice methodologies and state-of-the-art applications and tools in Performance Management. On the other hand, companies that have not performed as well recently would also make interesting case studies. Some examples are Nokia and Kodak.

Secondly, other less well-known organizations would also make interesting case studies, as they usually develop different and more innovative practices.

- Ajegroup. It is a Peruvian group which started in the Peruvian highlands as a small family business and which now runs on Asian, American and European markets.
- Interbank, a Peruvian bank which now operates around the world, but mainly in China.
- China Mobile was able to achieve the following results by using Performance Management measures, so the market share increased to over 72% and accounts for more than 70% of the whole market in China. It is through the mandatory introduction of China Mobile's KPIs that China Mobile has been able to have such success.
- www.moneysupermarket.com. It is the world's largest price comparison website based in the UK.
- Belron. It is the world's largest and fastest-growing vehicle glass repair and replacement company. They have had significant success through a combination of three measures to manage performance.
  - Total net conversions. How do we make sure that we capture work and deliver a satisfying job and get paid for it?
  - Net promoted score. They were able to grow customer delight through the application of that promoted score.
  - Operational excellence. It has enabled them to effectively manage at company level (they operate now in 34 countries) but also at branch

level.
- BIMBO. It is the world's biggest bakery company and is based in Mexico. It is an incredible example of Performance Management and the relationship with their labour force.
- TETRAPAK. It is a Swedish company and also a leading developer, manufacturer and marketer of packaging material, complete systems for processing, packaging and distribution for liquid food products. It is a good example of efficiency and focus strategy.

Thirdly, as governments tend to operate differently than profit organizations, they are also areas of interest in terms of case studies.

- Abu Dhabi Government. It has the inspiring vision to become one of the top five governments in the world. They have established a real state-of-the-art PM framework that is based on Balanced Scorecard.
- US Federal Government – The Office Personnel Management (OPM) oversees the employee Performance Management and has the whole system aligning all employees with federal performance.
- The State of California. The Tax Revenue Department and the Franchise Tax Board have had great achievements with their current Performance Management system.
- The State of Virginia. It uses Balanced Scorecards for a number of departments and agencies, where all processes are aligned with the goals, resulting in

effective people, programs and metrics.
- The Government of the Republic of Botswana.
- The Federal Republic of Ethiopia - The Ministry of Health.

7 Which are the main challenges of Performance Management in practice today?

The greatest challenge of Performance Management in practice today is the sheer complexity of the concept of Performance Management. Not only does Performance Management have multiple dimensions, but there is no best approach. Organizations of different types should not be doing everything in the same way. There are usually even multiple good alternatives for organizations of the same type. Furthermore, the continuous internationalisation of business means that Performance Management must take into consideration operations worldwide.

Another challenge is encouraging management to adopt a broader perspective on performance beyond just short-term financial results and to include the perspectives of other stakeholders in their consideration of what is good performance. However, many KPIs that assess the perspective of different stakeholders are intangible and therefore extremely difficult to measure accurately. Nevertheless, for organizations that have already realized this, the challenge would be to ensure that this underlying principle is reflected throughout the organization in terms of its

culture, its structure and processes.

Organizations have faced challenges implementing effective Performance Management system due to a lack of understanding and communication. There is the challenge itself to effectively explain

> Thirdly, as governments tend to operate differently than profit organizations, they are also an area of interest in terms of case studies.

the benefits of Performance Management systems. As a result, many organizations have a lack of motivation to explore such options. A lack of cooperation usually occurs due to the fear of making operations transparent and available to the scrutiny of outside parties. In addition, there are difficulties explaining to employees what exactly the process of implementing a Performance Management system is and how they can get involved. This lack of understanding of implementation can be attributed to the fact that research has generally focused on frameworks and measures. Therefore, there needs to be a stronger emphasis on design and implementation, followed by support and coaching.

8 What do you think should be improved in the use of Performance Management tools and processes?

Four major issues were raised in terms of Performance Management tools and processes; these can be clustered into four fields of:
- Tool and process interconnection, in order to evaluate everybody on similar metrics and creating corporate linkage.
- Flexibility of these tools towards cultures, economies and specific needs, in order to increase efficiency and for instance to focus on the developing markets.
- Analysis and automation that help measure synergy and priorities to benefit from networks and to isolate errors.
- Tools can be improved in regards to training, research and usage on staff level, which creates more sound data as well as processing capabilities.

9 What would you consider best practice in Performance Management?

Most of the interviewees saw clarity, transparency and shared definitions as key component of best practice in Performance Management. Furthermore, there was a strong emphasis on the need to view Performance Management as a long-term holistic, undertaking that needs alignment, the support and commitment of the organization on an ongoing basis. Measuring organizational maturity should thereby be the start of this holistic approach which should also leave space for intelligent feedback and a high volume of communication between all participants.

10 Which aspects of Performance Management should be emphasized during educational programs?

This question provoked substantial criticism on today's educational approach. In particular, critical thinking and the behavioural aspects and ways of thinking did not receive the attention they deserved in educational programs. In Performance Management, measuring the immeasurable needs creativity and imagination, innovation and a thorough understanding of the interrelations between processes, which is lacking in current educational programs.

One issue was the fact that students did not feel connected with the business world, which led them to suggest that educational programs should comprise of 60% study and 40% practice. Another suggestion was that education should focus more on teaching people about the use of performance information, rather than teaching them measurement frameworks or to increase the understanding of metrics and analysis.

Furthermore, although the importance of KPIs is undoubtable, students should also learn and understand that consumer satisfaction is the ultimate aim from which those KPIs should be derived. This is an interesting angle and may go in line with the bid for more research in educational programs.

11 What are the barriers to achieving higher levels of proficiency in Performance Management among practitioners?

Besides a few barriers on an operational level, the main issue are individual barriers. These are again caused by the lack of critical thinking and competency, in addition to the lack of integral methodologies and problems with offering a clear definition of positions and job duties. These barriers harm the management process and sometimes fail to allow simplicity and alignment.

The errors that occur at the operational level due to these barriers include short-sighted behaviour and the focus on operational instead of strategic results. Secondly, there is a lack of understanding within industry that Performance Management programs have to be able to rely on an intact and well organised governance system to create value.

In summary, one can see that training and unclear communication are key barriers and fields where further maturity is required for achieving effective Performance Management.

12.1 What Performance Management question would you like to have answered?

Based on the issues highlighted in previous questions, there seems to be a strong demand for future research in the area of Performance Management. On one hand there needs to be further research on the combination of measurable and non-measurable KPIs with respect to each other, as well at to time. On the other hand, research should investigate how to improve capabilities to redesign and enhance organizations, as well as managerial processes.

Specific questions regarding the direction that Performance Management should head towards include strategic planning or human resources and how Performance Management fits into the bigger picture. A standardized business process framework library would be beneficial to the field of Performance Management, especially regarding the demanded change in approach and view of the organization as a whole.

12.2 Which were the recent achievements in generating value from Performance Management in your organization?

Many participants of our survey found that the Performance Management systems they had implemented delivered substantial increases in measurable financial core figures. Not only was an increased in EBITDA noted, but empowerment, an increase in focus and excellent employee incentives were noted as results along with increased accountability and alignment. Whilst there may have been a noticeable slowdown at the end of implementing changes, these will start affecting the vitality and enthusiasm of staff and on the long-run shareholders returns will improve. This is not true only for private enterprises, but also for government departments, especially in states where Performance Management systems existed throughout the state.

12.3 As a consultant, what are the most common issues that your customers raised related to Performance Management?

When consultants engage with clients there seems to be a discrepancy between the levels of insight between both parties in regards to the Performance Management process. Customers see the steps needed as short-term and an isolated engagement, whereas consultants know that this does not hold true and that the first step is to broaden the understanding of the client. In addition, at the operational level, concerns were raised about the issue of holding individuals accountable from the organizational level as well as about the problem of how to manage change and motivate employees towards a performance culture.

13 We are developing a database of Performance Management subjects and degrees in Performance Management. What are your suggestions relevant to the database (i.e. subjects or degrees such as the Masters in Managing Organizational Performance)?

Although opinions where diverse, there was consensus that the alignment needed to be achieved between the paradigm, the philosophical framework of studying organizations and KPIs. This should be measured with individual KPIs, as well as with organizational ones. Additionally, some responses suggested that the students and teachers should help with assessing the value of courses for the individual.

Practitioner Perspectives

From the perspective of interviewed practitioners, Performance Management represents a complex process of aligning organizational strategy and people to that strategy, an organization's purpose to move forward. It is driven by actual implementation of a system in the organization, combined with innovation, service excellence and efficiency, along with KPIs.

Practitioners have different views when it comes to levels of Performance Management, but they all agree that the relationship between these levels is essential, by means of integration. For example, some see it from the point of view of variable salary (see Mabrouk Aib interview, page 27), whereas others consider it the blood running through the veins of the organization (see Dr. Ahmed Samy interview, page 23). In the case of public organizations, whose roles are somewhat different, Performance Management is about choosing the right KPIs and using them in the appropriate way. The 2012 Performance Management trends mentioned by practitioners were the development of strategy, in the private and public sector, business intelligence, automation of Performance Management Systems, as well as the acknowledgement of benefits of all opportunities.

From a practical perspective, research should focus more on Performance Management in the context of organizational culture, process automation, strategy alignment and, according to some (see Jodi Traversaro interview, page 33), on implementing a Performance Management System in public institutions, where the management style is different.

Measuring performance is, as most practitioners agree, faced with significant challenges. One of them is the lack of a formal strategy, applied at all levels, not just by the upper management, put together in a clear management system. In addition, the complexity of managing performance makes it difficult to align strategy across levels and to keep a satisfying degree of feedback and cooperation. In public service organizations, the challenges are even greater, as leaders in government, for example, need to be formed as such when it comes to Performance Management and because the context of such an organization is different than in the private sector. This makes it hard to measure performance, especially when the impact of a public institution is often far broader.

When asked about what they consider to be best practices in the field, practitioners outlined the measurement of organizational maturity, the use of Balanced Scorecard and a stable and clear plan which should be followed by open minded teams. Concerning the development of educational programs, practitioners support the emphasis on critical thinking and systemic approaches, a more pragmatic approach to theory, as well as to KPIs and a higher level of acknowledgement of employees as the core of the system.

From the practitioners' points of view, Performance Management is an intricate process which needs to be adapted according to the context of the organization. Whether it is public or private, there is a need for more formality in applying strategy, for example in the form of a worldwide database to enable standardized process framework. ▣

Academic Perspectives

From the academic angle, Performance Management gives great importance to strong alignment in an organization, of both performance at different levels and the characteristics of that performance, based on the efficacy, efficiency, effectiveness, ethics and aesthetics, the 5 Es (see Ricardo Rodriguez-Ulloa interview, page 43).

Current trends of Performance Management are directed, among others, towards the way the human factor is included when measuring performance. For example, there is interest in knowing how non-financial KPIs are and will be used to measure financial aspects. A growing level of acknowledgement concerning the importance of considering human aspects in the context of Performance Management was also noted. This leads to the development of different types of KPIs, which reflect not only the human approach as part of the scientific one, but also the global issues and the synergy between the hard and the soft – the science and the person.

Research should focus on building better systems of measuring and integrating KPIs. These systems need to be supported by systemic thinking and adequate technologies. To complete this view, the need to modify the current principles and methodologies of Performance Management should be addressed, so as to fit the needs and views of the next generation of workforce. Moreover, research should use not only the examples of high-performing companies, such as Facebook and Google, but also those of under-performing organizations, like Nokia and Kodak. Regarding aspects which need improvement, opinions vary. Some think that Performance Management products should be better understood before acquired and applied, whereas other views state that the use of tools at an individual level, including the feedback process is the most important aspect to be improved, thus making effective communication one of the best practices in the field (see Sujay Nair interview, page 16).

From the academic perspective, educational programs should emphasize on teaching students how the principles and theories of Performance Management can and are applied in real-life situations. This should be done by developing students' critical thinking, spirit of innovation and systemic thinking, adapted to the current global contexts. One important barrier standing in the way of successful Performance Management implementations is the financial aspect. Many organizations seem to be bound by financial objectives and the capital markets, which leads to a lack of integration between the financial and operations areas of an organization. In addition, there is a lack of critical thinking and of smart technologies to support performance measurement.

At last, in developing educational programs on Performance Management, it would be important to create an overview of the programs' quality, by offering a detailed profile of both the professors and the students taking up each subject. Also, programs should focus more on the alignment between the criteria of measuring performance and the actual KPIs, as well as on aligning an organization's overall KPIs with the individual ones. ▪

Consultant Perspectives

From the point of view of consultants, Performance Management should, first of all, be distinguished from performance measurement which implies more focus on KPIs, rather than on the strategy itself. Also, Performance Management represents the correct management of resources available, in order to achieve organizational objectives.

In the public sector, what drives interest in Performance Management is mainly the impact on society, as well as the setting of manageable and attainable targets. However, in both the private and public sector, clarity is an essential driver of success. Concerning Performance Management at organizational levels, an interesting aspect is brought forward by one practitioner - performance architecture (see Alan Meekings interview, page 29). Performance Management systems cover all areas and levels of a company and include all logical processes enabling decision making. Commitment, passion and full involvement are some of the others aspects mentioned.

One of this year's trends in Performance Management includes a concept called Connected Performance and which is comprised of four parts: Performance Architecture, Performance Exploration, Performance Planning and Performance Culture (see Alan Meekings interview, page 30). When it comes to research, consultants agree that what needs more analysis is generally leadership and the process of leading others. Since there is a misconception that people who are promoted must have the needed leadership skills, it is important to control the flow of work and to stay on course of your leadership plan. In this context, BIMBO, TETRAPAK and MoneySupermarket are considered to be examples of good leadership and healthy Performance Management.

Nowadays, globalization is seen by some consultants as a challenge, since it makes Performance Management difficult to standardize, especially if an organization operates on different markets in different countries. This challenge is often completed by insufficient levels of motivation, mobilization and communication. One of the best practices to overcome these challenges is a good strategy implementation which takes into consideration the diversity of human resources across the world.

Regarding how Performance Management is taught, consultants believe that educational programs should emphasize more on leadership and information management, in the context of reality and real-life situations.

One issue related to Performance Management is the fact that sometimes people are overwhelmed by the amount of data and they need advice on how to organize everything, using the right tools. Other issues raised are about the impact of strategy of obtaining performance results on Research & Development investments, as well as about the lack of competition. ▦

Interviews

The following interviews are alphabetically arranged with regards to the interviewee's surname.

Interviewee name:
Sujay Nair
Title:
Lecturer
Main subjects:
Enterprise Performance Management
Strategic Management Accounting
Organization:
The University of Melbourne
Country:
Australia
Continent:
Australia

1. What does the term Performance Management mean to you?

It is a very broad term. For me, I would say, Performance Management is comprised of a collection of principles, tools and techniques to help an organization achieve its objectives.

2. What drives interest in Performance Management?

The reason why there is a strong interest in Performance Management is because of its strong links to the organization's ability to achieve its objectives. Organizations use the principles, tools and techniques of Performance Management to ensure that the purpose of their existence is fulfilled.

3. What are your thoughts on the relationship between Performance Management at organizational, departmental and individual level?

In an ideal environment, a high performing individual should lead to a high performing department. And a high performing department should lead to a high performing organization. There should be a very strong link. In reality, it sometimes doesn't happen in that way because of leakages. I think the most common leakage happens because the objectives of each of these components are not aligned. So even though a person is doing his job and achieving his or her performance objectives, it does not translate into the department achieving its goals and objectives because they are not consistent, and so on and so forth. The other source of leakage, in addition to the misaligned objectives, is the lack of leadership capabilities. So although a person is really doing well in his job, the leadership at the department and/or organization level is not able to translate a good performance at the individual level to good performance at the departmental and /or organizational level.

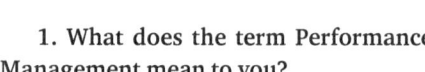

The reason why there is a strong interest in Performance Management is because of its strong links to the organization's ability to achieve its objectives. Organizations use the principles, tools and techniques of Performance Management to ensure that the purpose of their existence is fulfilled.

4. What are the 2012 key trends in Performance Management from the perspective of your knowledge and experience in this field?

One of the trends is the broadening of performance considerations beyond the shareholders' perspective. So when one looks at how an organization is performing, one is not just confining oneself to the shareholders, but also asking the question on how it is performing in the eyes of the employees, local communities, global communities and so on and so forth. So I think this is one important trend.

Another trend would be the recognition of the behavioral elements and human biases in Performance Management. So although we have certain tools or techniques that in theory should work in a certain way, and because human beings are not always rational and are subject to biases, the actual results could be different. These behavioral aspects which affect the way people act in the real world may cause one to reconsider some of the Performance Management principles and/or tools that are used.

5. What aspects of Performance Management should be explored more through research?

Going back to what I mentioned about the first trend in 2012, we need more research on what is the right way to measure performance in a broader sense. So instead of just measuring shareholders' returns, where we have a lot of theory and experience in doing, how does one measure 'returns' to the employees, local communities, global communities?

Another interesting topic that would potentially benefit from more research is whether the principles, tools and techniques that we have in Performance Management need to be modified for the new generation that has recently joined the workforce, Generation Y. The hypothesis is that Generation Y has very different needs and wants compared to Generation X and also to baby boomers. Therefore there could be a need to modify principles, tools and techniques we have been using to manage performance.

6. Please provide some examples of organizations which you would recommend for study due to their approach to Performance Management

and achievements.

I think companies that have performed well recently, like Google and Facebook are interesting to study. In addition, companies that have performed continuously well and managed to sustain that performance level over a long period of time, like IBM and GE, would also be interesting. On the other hand, underperforming companies like Nokia and Kodak are also interesting to study to highlight paths that management should avoid. Having said this, it is quite likely that many, if not all of these organizations have already been studied by researchers and academics.

7. Which are the main challenges of Performance Management in practice today?

The challenge is to encourage management to adopt a broader perspective on performance beyond just short-term financial results and to include the perspectives of other stakeholders in their consideration of what is good performance. For those organizations that have already realized this, the challenge would be to ensure that this underlying principle is reflected throughout the organization in terms of its culture, its structure, and processes, this is one of the challenges faced by organizations today.

8. What do you think should be improved in the use of Performance Management tools and processes?

One area that we can do better is the way the Performance Management tools are used. For example, in the case of individual performance, based on my observations, I believe that the quality of the discussion that happens during performance evaluation dialogues can be improved. Does the supervisor commit enough time to have a thorough discussion? Does the supervisor ask the tough questions when performance is below expectations? Does the supervisor get at the root cause of the underperformance? Does the supervisor give the person evaluated concrete steps on how they can improve their performance going forward? Does the supervisor provide informal feedback frequently, and not just once or twice per year - to give the person opportunity to improve his/her performance and

ensure there are no surprises when formal performance ratings are handed out?

9. What would you consider best practice in Performance Management?

I know of an organization that has a very robust individual performance evaluation approach. In this organization it was not uncommon to have informal monthly performance conversations between the individual and his/her supervisor. However, formal evaluation took place every six months. So these frequent informal discussions around performance ensured there were no surprises when it came to the bi-annual formal evaluation. The supervisors spent significant amount of time doing these performance evaluations, which in turn sent a signal that it was a very important thing to get right and added credibility to the process. As part of the formal evaluation process, the supervisor typically spoke to between 8 and 15 different people who worked with the employee to get a sense on how he/she is performing. Once the performance is calibrated across a similar cohort of employees, the supervisor will then have the formal performance dialogue with the employee. This dialogue will cover both the strengths and developmental areas for him. Employees were encouraged to find ways to leverage on their strengths as making

> The challenge is to encourage management to adopt a broader perspective on performance beyond just short-term financial results and to include the perspectives of other stakeholders in their consideration of what is good performance.

full use of these "spikes" would be crucial in succeeding in this organization. Time was also spent talking about the developmental areas of the employees and the steps he/she could take, with the supervisor's support, to improve in these areas. The supervisor had to ensure that these developmental areas were made known to the employee in no uncertain terms, but at the same time were not over emphasized, at the expense of his/her strengths.

10. Which aspects of Performance Management should be emphasized during educational programs?

Going back to the definition of Performance Management, I suppose that educational programs should focus on the most important principles, tools and techniques that are currently used. So it would be important to cover these in the class. In addition, real life examples of how organizations use these principles, tools and techniques should also be highlighted in class.

11. What are the barriers to achieving higher levels of proficiency in Performance Management among practitioners?

I think one of the most important barriers is the overemphasis by capital markets on short-term financial results. The pressure for companies to announce quarterly earnings and guidance, and the level of emphasis analysts place on these announcements encourage the companies to think short-term to the detriment of its longer term objectives and performance.

12. What Performance Management question would you like to have answered?

I think this is similar to what was asked before in question 5 – therefore my answers here would be the same.

13. We are developing a database of Performance Management subjects and degrees in Performance Management. What are your suggestions relevant to the database (i.e. subjects or degreed such as the Masters in Managing Organizational Performance)?

I presume the database would include the name of the organization offering these courses, the type of subjects or the course being offered (Masters vs. Bachelor's degree etc.), how long it would take, the costs involved, the topics that would be covered and so on and so forth. It would also be good to have the following two pieces of information (if not already covered in the database). First, a fairly detailed profile of the academic/lecturer involved in delivering the subject and second, the profile of students who would be in the class. I think these 2 pieces of information will be important determinants of the quality of the program.

Interviewee name:
Dr. Feng Cai Qiu/Frank Qiu
Title:
-Executive Director/Senior Partner
-Chief Expert of HR Management
-Expert of Performance Management
Researcher of Global
Telecommunication Talent Management
Organization:
Singapore Empower Consulting Group
Pty., Ltd.
Country:
China
Continent:
Asia

Overview

1. What does the term Performance Management mean to you?

Different groups understand the concept of "Performance Management" in different ways. In China, the different concepts are combined and selected in order to suit the political and environmental conditions before putting them into practice. According to my research in Europe and North America on the practice of Performance Management in China, I think several features should be mentioned: First, from the group perspective, Performance Management is a synergy of individual, family and organization. The cooperation and effect among these three parties contributes to a sustained high performance in an organization. Second, Performance Management is an integral activity. From the vision and target design to the process control, to result evaluation and then to the final achievement, the whole process is a closed circle. People in China generally accept this point of view. Third, from the finance perspective, Performance Management is a control system. The CEO treats it as a system in which different strategies can be applied and implemented; HR treats it as a tool which can explore employees' abilities to achieve their targets, allowing them to cooperate with the organization; employees treat this as a tool which can make their work clearer, more organized through a higher degree of planning.

Thus, in China, the concept of Performance Management varies with different people; each approach has value in practice and is feasible. When it comes to the group's point of view, from the Performance Management's essence and processes to its role on management decisions, we should consider it from different angles..

2. What drives interest in Performance Management?

In reality, the Chinese public is not interested in this topic, it is actually quite critical of it. HR might be interested, and the researchers may be more interested in it. Most of the staff has a negative feeling towards Performance Management, and leaders in industries are not interested in it.

> Most of the staff has a negative feeling towards Performance Management, and leaders in industries are not interested in it. According to our survey within China, nearly 50% of the employees and organizations have low recognition and satisfaction towards Performance Management.

According to our survey within China, nearly 50% of the employees and organizations have low recognition and satisfaction towards Performance Management.

Personally speaking, I am very interested in this topic because I am both a researcher and a practitioner, and I am also an expert who promotes this concept in China. I think that Performance Management is helpful to individuals, families and organizations since I practice it myself and have experienced its benefits. That is the reason why I do it. However, in China, the concept has not been driven, instead, there is more pain, resentment, resistance and rejection.

3. What are your thoughts on the relationship between Performance Management at organizational, departmental and individual level?

I do not agree with some of the arguments put forward by Western countries on Performance Management. Their process involves setting goals at the organizational level, then breaking them down at the departmental level, followed by having the departments complete the goals and missions by way of allocating tasks to sectors and finally passing them down to the employees. As a result, the goal of the entire organization can only be achieved if the individual staff members complete the tasks that are assigned to them. I think that this method of Performance Management is only half of the picture.

In China, the other half relates to relationship dynamics; it is impossible to make a conclusion as to whether it should be the individual priority or the organizational priorities, because sometimes individual Performance Management is superior to organizational Performance Management. In this case, when designing a Performance Management system, we should use the bottom-up method instead of top-down one, which means the organization is at the mercy of Performance Management at the individual level. In this case, the organization needs to do some adjustments and optimizations according to the individual needs, goals and internal commitments. By doing this, the entire organization can achieve high performance and organizational goals.

From this perspective, in order to ultimately achieve the organizational performance, individual performance, should be a focus. This relationship is often present in the high-tech and traditional businesses. This is especially important now for a number of reasons: "career boredom" from people who started their careers in the 1980s and

1990s, the impact of the Internet economy, the talent diversity and individuality, and the seamless exchange of knowledge promote the relationships among staff.

This means that the Performance Management system among the individual, departmental and organizational levels has become increasingly complex. It is not simply individuals at the mercy of the organization or vice versa. In the international arena, I think this relationship will become increasingly diverse and personalized. Therefore, we need to model ourselves to companies that are already doing this.

For some large state-owned enterprises in China, employees obey the department and the department obeys the organization from the enterprise, central, provincial and prefectural level. However, for the grass-roots enterprises which are under the prefecture level, if they want to achieve high performance, most of the time the departments are required to obey the individuals. When the individuals are subordinate to the organizations, a clearer symbiotic relationship exists.

So in China, we need to consider the relationships according to different levels, groups, industries and organizational maturities. Grass-roots employees are more adaptive and can go with the flow; therefore, the use of Performance Management should be in an open environment. In this environment, the relationship between individuals, departments and organizations is relatively casual; while individuals still obey the department and the department still obeys the organization, the organization is more receptive to suggestions put forward at the departmental level and similarly the departmental to the individual level. This is symbiotic relationship. For organizations which are in a non-market environment, they are in a very traditional organizational environment, so there is very clearly a top-down relationship there.

Research

4. What are the 2012 key trends in Performance Management from the perspective of your knowledge and experience in this field?

I think there are a few points you

may want to consider: firstly, from the central and the national point of view, the concept of and practice of Performance Management will continue to be valued and enhanced. Last year, Premier Wen proposed to strengthen the reform of Performance Management in government, and also piloted the idea in Shenzhen, Shanghai and Xiamen. From the SASAC (State-owned Assets Supervision and Administration Commission) perspective, SASAC has asked more than 150 state-owned enterprises to carry out the implementation of a Performance Management system.

In the private sector, because of market competition and financial crisis, improving basic operations and improving their work quality and efficiency, are two reasons why they also strengthen Performance Management. From the education system, the Performance Management is perpetually being improved and refined. There are more and more scholars considering individual differences when they study Performance Management. Thus, from the academic point of view, Performance Management is increasingly popular.

Secondly, from the entire technological environment point of view, there are three parts worth mentioning.

1. Balanced Scorecard gained a lot of promotion in the past few years, but there are plenty of problems that came out during the

process of promotion. I did research in the University of Nottingham and Cambridge in England, and I also communicated with Dr. Kaplan, the professor at Harvard University. I found that many Chinese enterprises had problems when they were using the Balanced Scorecard. They began to doubt the practicality of the Balanced Scorecard in China. This is also my PhD research topic. After much research and investigation, I

found that Chinese organizations casted doubt on the application of the BSC and started thinking about how to improve the BSC in order to adapt it to the Chinese environment better. This also means the technology and ideas behind its logic required some adjustments. China now has already begun research in this area, and I am also looking for a suitable BSC.

2. The application of KPIs in the technical fields is not enough. In Britain, Professor Neely in Cranfield School has published a book named "Performance Prism". This theory is rarely known by people in China, because there are not enough people who are interested in learning, understanding and applying this theory. Therefore, it is not as popular as the Balanced Scorecard in China and there are not many people putting it to use.

3. China is still using the DuPont method. In financial management applications, organizations assess business performance by decomposing the original DuPont index to set KPI targets. In addition, the Chinese state-owned enterprises are primarily using EVA in evaluating the performance. China is still using this method, and is still improving upon it.

4. Whether Chinese organizations can make the Balanced Scorecard, KPIs and traditional EVA assessment to align and to evaluate different levels of employees within an organization. For example, the strategic level may adopt the BSC, the departmental level may use KPIs and the staff level may create a new model to evaluate what is detailed, but staff growth and development can still occur while maintaining the company's vision and financial objectives, despite having different PM tools being used. Currently, the demand of Performance Management at the technical level is very high. However, it is hard to say whether the study that involves hierarchical classification of different Performance Management systems would be successful or not. I have done a lot of research in this area, and created the models to explore a suitable Performance Management system to our employees. This system should be different from the Balanced Scorecard, the EVA and the complicated KPIs, it can track staff to help them concentrate on their future and their personal development,

> I do not agree with some of the arguments put forward by Western countries on Performance Management. [...] When designing a Performance Management system, we should use the bottom-up method instead of top-down one, which means the organization is at the mercy of Performance Management at the individual level.

helping them to reach their individual dreams and needs, which can stimulate enterprises to reach sustainable, higher levels of performance while at the same time improve the efficiency of the process. How to incorporate these comprehensive factors together, which are the past, the present and the future, the financial and non-financial systems, the leading and lagging indicators, are also mentioned by Kaplan in the Balanced Scorecard concept.

More and more people in China require a new system to be designed to suit the employee level. The third trend is the group in China that will pay close attention to Performance Management. In 2012, the foreign-funded enterprises will focus less on Performance Management, because they have incorporated it as a part of their quality management system. However, I think more people in state-owned enterprises will be concerned about Performance Management, because they are facing competition and internationalization and they don't want to lose their momentum in the global financial environment. Therefore, more managers and HR departments will pay attention to Performance Management in the state-owned enterprises level and in the employee level. In addition, the degree of concern in private enterprises in 2012 will also be improved, but not as much as the state-owned enterprises. Private enterprises are also not completely out of the impact of financial crisis. The state-owned enterprises do not have such problems, and they only need to focus on development and expansion. Therefore they need have suitable Performance Management in the aspects of technology, management and innovation.

In terms of the academic field, they will shift their attention from the strategic level to the technical and theoretical research on the staff-level. There has been too much research on the strategic level worldwide but too little attention payed to individual Performance Management in a more diverse society. In China, the individual environment is experiencing a turbulent time, and the employees' ideological values have not yet fully formed; many scholars and experts may not be aware of this fact and know how to design a Performance Management system for those employees who have not formed their own dominant values. This is not only relevant to China, but also to the world. In the future, it will be a trend and also a challenge to study Performance Management in a diverse, intricate and flexible environment.

5. What aspects of Performance Management should be explored more through research?

I think Performance Management should be studied more from an individual human level more than a technical, group level. This is the paradigm shift academics need. For example, when I was doing academic research in the United Kingdom and the United States, I found that even though the application and implementation of Performance Management systems in enterprises are identical to that in a Chinese context, their results are higher

In the Chinese context, effective Performance Management is difficult to achieve because of the lack of free competition and the difficulty to leave a company.

and better than that of China. This is because their culture matches the theory. In China however, the human environment has several characteristics that need to be considered.

First, study the effect of China's political influence on the enterprise, and the associated workplace satisfaction, employment, values and professional ideology from the perspective of the Chinese people. This idea directly impacts on staff's concept of employment and their judgment on their success. In European countries, this perception has been formed, while in China, it is still blank. Therefore, in the human environment, in the application and implementation of Performance Management we need a breakthrough.

Second is the research on the enterprise environment. In China, the ecological environment increasingly affects the execution and implementation of Performance Management. This ecological environment includes presidents. The presidents in Chinese enterprises and in foreign-funded enterprises are not the same: general managers in China are not determined by the market, or the shareholders, or the business performance.

Therefore, the study of how leaders affect Performance Management and whether there is a Performance Management system suitable for Chinese environment, this subject will be more and more important.

Third, study the changes in the staff's mentality, especially the difference between 80-90s and 50-60s. There is a huge change and conflict on the outlooks on life, values, career outlook and personalized view within these 30 years. This change in Western countries occurred over the space of 100 years. Following in the ideological background of traditional Chinese culture, the traditional business leaders (who were born in 1950s-1960s) have plenty of conflict with their employees (who were born in 1980s-1990s). This conflict will affect the design of Performance Management systems, coordination and matching, and to promote a balance between employers and employees inside the organization.

Fourth, I'm doing a study of the harmonious development of Performance Management. China raised three slogans: a rapid and healthy development, to create a harmonious environment and education reform. Researchers in Performance Management should study how to get individuals, families and organizations to cooperate and respond to the characteristics of China's development. In Kaplan's theory, the relationship between staff, organization and customer is coordinated very well. There are still some criticism that the theory has no synergy to role of the government, suppliers, buyers and other interested persons. In China, I will be researching more in the collaborative management of individuals, families and organizations, since they represent different customer needs. At present, the government also proposed this need, and both businesses and ordinary people need a harmonious, healthy and happy organization. Performance Management is an entry point and we have the opportunity to explore how we can design a system that encourages better performance.

6. Please provide some examples of organizations which you would recommend for study due to their approach to Performance Management and achievements.

Currently, we can't say China has a

successful case. I've been a performance consultant in China Mobile for 10 years. Upon utilizing Performance Management concepts and frameworks, China Mobile was able to reach a higher level, but not a very successful level. China Mobile achieved results in three aspects by using Performance Management. First, it improved the market coverage from top to bottom, and its market share is over 72% now in China. Second, its revenue market share accounted for more than 70% of the whole market in China. These two indicators show China Mobile's improvement on its financial performance through Performance Management. Third, through the pressure transmission of Performance Management, China Mobile pushed the Chinese mobile communication industry to greater heights. Communication used to be a luxury, while now almost everyone in China has a cell phone. This is not because something the telecommunications industry brought about. It was actually caused by the mandatory introduction of China Mobile's KPIs. China Mobile made every employee take a top-down market penetration approach, which meant focusing from the city to the countryside, then to the children. This mechanism promotes the development of the Chinese communication industry to the world and the upgrading of the Chinese people's quality of life in the modern era.

Practice

7. Which are the main challenges of Performance Management in practice today?

The challenges in government departments, state-owned enterprises, foreign-funded enterprises and private enterprise are not the same. But they also have some basic commonalities.

First, the political environment in China for Performance Management is not very mature.

Second, the soil for China to implement Performance Management also needs to be cultivated. This soil refers to the human resources market, which requires fair, free and open competition, and this in China is not yet fully formed. Therefore, the concept of "fair competition and survival of the fittest" of Performance Management is quite difficult to achieve, and Performance Management can not play its proper role in China. For example, in foreign companies the Balanced Scorecard is used as an important tool to do staff classification in order to promote fair competition, while this situation is difficult to achieve in China. This is because Chinese companies can not let employees leave the company, or dismiss unsatisfactory employees. China does not exist in this environment, because Chinese employees are formal workers who cannot be dismissed easily. Human resources market in foreign countries is a free market; it is a two-way voluntary relationship. Therefore, in the Chinese context, effective Performance Management is difficult to achieve because of the lack of free competition and the difficulty to leave a company.

Third, the level of professionalism in the application Performance Management needs to be upgraded. In fact, many

> I use Performance Management in my family, and I also encourage all the employees in my company to use it. Encouraging every employee use the concept of Performance Management to build a harmonious, happy and healthy family to stimulate them to work more efficiently is what I practice.

business owners, managers and employees apply Performance Management not in its original form, but rather relate it to the company's variety of professional capacity system, for instance, incentive management, targets management, practice management, application systems, and docking new systems. The ability of professional managers in these areas is still lacking. Therefore, Performance Management is not a single system, but is required to supplement other systems. Hence, it requires professional managers to have a stronger ability to apply strict Performance Management frameworks and China is still in progress. Fourth, the Performance Management system in China is different from what is in foreign countries that pay more attention to the rules and systems. Therefore, in foreign countries, when the Performance Management system is used in the enterprise, there is system interaction and this interaction results in the desired effect of Performance Management. However in China, regardless of the state-owned enterprises or private enterprises, many systems are still building. Therefore, when linking Performance Management to immature systems, the effect will be affected. Many people are still wary and don't understand how Performance Management can be used to the benefit of the individual and the enterprise.

8. What do you think should be improved in the use of Performance Management tools and processes?

Each person's point of view should be different. With regards to the Balanced Scorecard in China, the biggest problem does not concern human resources, and does not imply rigid and flexible combination within human resources. The biggest advantage of the Balanced Scorecard is the effective integration of operational systems and financial systems. I think this is Kaplan's contribution. So when a business is in need of operating systems and financial systems designed for organizational effectiveness, promoting the organization of sustainable development, this theory will play a role. So it is necessary to identify what kind of companies will have this type of problem. But when the focus of a business, at some stages is in the human resources or marketing, the BSC may not be the best tool. Although BSC also mentions the link between human resources, it only focuses on the association among the disciplines. How to use it in specific environment, what difficulties will be met during implementation and what features the human resources will have under different situations, those questions are waiting for in-depth study.

There are a plenty of cases and examples in the practice of using BSC in operational systems and financial systems, but considerably fewer in the case of human resources. The primary segment in the Kaplan case study is reform at the strategic and application levels in the 12 enterprises which are primarily located in Europe and America. However, the practice and exploration on human resources aspect needs to be increased. In addition, he did not take into account the difference between the human resources environment in Asia. Therefore, I also explore the application of the BSC in the Asian region, which needs to focus on the human resource management theory. In addition, the BSC does not take the psychological factors into account. It is more concerned with the overall organization's application and day-to-day operations, but not concerned about each employee's sustained growth and motivation. Although it is also known as the Staff Balanced Scorecard, its operation and logic aren't focused on the psychological point of view, but rather on the financial perspective. Therefore, the BSC needs to be improved on the staff level. Globally, the successful Personal Balanced Scorecard theory is from an American named Lecsion, who made a number of theories that really resonate with me. In his view point, the starting point of the Balanced Scorecard is "empowerment", and the ending point is "finance". In China, I think this theory could be continued to be studied and improved.

China uses KPIs very often, and three points need to be improved: First, how to improve KPI usage in collaborative departments. This is a short-term key focus for KPIs. The biggest advantage of it is the vertical transmission, but it is relatively weak on the correlation of horizontal value transfer. Second, many administrative departments can not use KPIs to quantify their performance, because they have trouble measuring immeasurable things. Third, distinguishing the lagging and leading KPIs and let staff perceive them correctly, as well as creating a corporate linkage design is also difficult. Fourth, KPIs and BSC are becoming IT-oriented, which means to get efficiency improvement from the support of IT systems in order to reduce the influence of human factors, China also needs to be upgraded in this aspect.

9. What would you consider best practice in Performance Management?

The best practice should be at home. Bring BSC into families in order to create a harmonious and happy atmosphere in the family. I use Performance Management in my family, and I also encourage all the employees in my company to use it. Encouraging every employee use the concept of Performance Management to build a harmonious, happy and healthy family to stimulate them to work more efficiently is what I practice. It can also delay the departure of employees. To achieve the collaboration between employees, families and organizations, the employees in our company are a good example. In addition, as I mentioned before, China Mobile is also a good practice.

Education

10. Which aspects of Performance Management should be emphasized during educational programs?

First, the national environment should be emphasized, which means how to design Performance Management systems under this country's political environment. Secondly, organizational culture and the ecological environment will directly affect the practice of Performance Management theory. We need to study how different cultures are embedding the design and implementation of Performance Management systems, for instance, how to combine the human environment and the living environment of Chinese enterprises to make the Performance Management more practical. Thirdly, the theory of Performance Management should be understood from practice, experienced and then summarized. In my opinion, university undergraduate and postgraduate students should be "60% study, 40% practice", in order to really understand the practical science. This is my proposal for Performance Management education. For example, for a two-year EMBA, nine months should be used for practicing, so as to cultivate the demonstration of Performance Management capabilities. I raised 30 Performance Management capabilities and these capabilities must be proved through demonstration in order to become a qualified human resources student. In addition, on this basis, students must have a clear understanding on what are the specific projects of Performance Management capabilities. Take the 30 capabilities for example, we should tell students what they are, how to cultivate them, where can the students get the training for them and by using which way. When the students are qualified, which level they can reach, and what extent of work they can deal with after they go into the society. I hope those aspects could be emphasized because this applied talents are what China and the world welcome.

11. What are the barriers to achieving higher levels of proficiency in Performance Management among practitioners?

Firstly, the organizational culture. The culture of performance implementation directly impacts the effect of an organizational performance execution. Performance culture includes the degree of recognition, competition, sense of fairness, identity and cooperation. A healthy performance culture is very important. Secondly, the science and differentiation of a Performance Management operating system. The science applies to different enterprises and different departments using different Performance Management systems. The differentiation means different departments should have different characteristics; therefore, they should use corresponding models to match their features. This is the scientific nature of Performance Management operating systems, which requires more targeting and differentiation, because it will directly affect the implementation of Performance Management. Many failures in China are due to the lack of consideration in these features at the designing stage. Thirdly, the ability in the full Performance Management training and the level of application eligibility that will directly affect the implementation of Performance Management. The Performance Management application level in China now is not high enough. Foreign-funded enterprises may be higher and private enterprises are in the middle. Therefore, we need to train a large number of professional managers in the capability of Performance Management. Fourthly, the implementation

> The Performance Management application level in China now is not high enough. Foreign-funded enterprises may be higher and private enterprises are in the middle. Therefore, we need to train a large number of professional managers in the capability of Performance Management.

of Performance Management is a long-term behavior, which should be gradually optimized and promoted.

Specific question

Practitioner

Which were the recent achievements in generating value from Performance Management in your organization?

From the staff's point of view, first of all, the work structure is better meaning that the work will be more focused. Excellent employee incentives increase. Second of all, the number for excellent employees increases; the better they do their job, the greater return they will get. However, to the medium and poorly performing staff,

Performance Management deprives them of their rights and interests.

From the company's point of view, through the operation of this system the company can, firstly, promote the establishment of long-term development concepts. By building such a system, long-term positive behavior in a company is increased. Secondly, the vitality of the organization will be raised. The activity may drop when Performance Management is just introduced into the company, however, the vitality will increase after a period of time. This vitality is mainly reflected in the business operations and it refers to the enthusiasm of the staff. Thirdly, in the long-run, after two or three years of

introduction, the returns to shareholders will be increased, particularly for those enterprises which mandatorily implement Performance Management.

The Human Resources management can reach a higher level and have a stronger sense of accountability because the requirement on improving their professional standards is stronger. Before Performance Management is carried out, job challenges are relatively high. After implementation, the problems are highlighted, promoting the human resources to enhance the professionalism, and a change in the role from an affairs expert to a consultant expert. ▦

Interviewee name:
Ahmed Samy
Title:
Director – Corporate Strategy Office
Organization:
Western Region Municipality, Abu Dhabi
Country:
UAE
Region:
Middle East

1. What does the term Performance Management mean to you?

What does Performance Management mean to me? I'll try to answer your questions very briefly and simply, Performance Management to me is about understanding where the organization stands today and monitoring how it is going to achieve whatever future it sets for itself. So, understanding is key but also embedding improvement opportunities so that you know that your trend is always moving up, there is no value in Performance Management if you stay where you are, so that's what really Performance Management means to me and I'm referring to corporate Performance Management, I'm not just referring to individual Performance Management because there's always a confusion between the two.

What I'm saying is that Individual Performance Management is only a

component of Corporate Performance Management. Without improving, you're not managing your performance because this is not just about recording, this is not just about monitoring, this is about managing the whole cycle and a very important part of that cycle is to assess where you are, review it and then make decisions to improve. Without that piece, it's not really Performance Management, it loses the value.

2. What drives interest in Performance Management?

Simple, straightforward answer to this question- I wouldn't appreciate any manager that wouldn't want to know how is he performing and how his team's performing

and how his function is performing and how his business unit is performing. I wouldn't see that as a manager, this is why I'm also convinced that Performance Management is a key skill in any management.

Now, organizations are basically a group of individuals who are working together for a certain cause. From the same perspective, the CEO of any organization knows, "how is he doing, how is he performing?" As an organization and as an individual the link is always there.

So the interest is there, if I would rephrase the question, I wouldn't be asking the interest, because you wouldn't find anyone saying, "I'm not interested in Performance Management", but you would see somebody saying, "I might see Performance Management as actually a core thing to do", or "I might see it is as a preferred thing to do, more likely must have vs. prefer to have". That is where organizations lie within those key perspectives and as you move from preferred to have to must have you mature as an organization. So regardless of the size of the organization at the start, whether it's a small business or a big corporation, they wouldn't focus much attention on Performance Management. They usually tend to move towards operations, you know, on-the-ground stuff and forget about Performance Management or lose sight of it. As they mature, they start learning that they have been doing something, but they haven't really been monitoring what they were doing properly. There also could be

> Performance Management is the framework; it's like the blood running in the veins of the organization.

some situations where they might see no improvement, just the status quo and this is going to start driving more interest and considering it as a core business. Pretty much anyone who's involved in Performance Management knows that this is not something that has definitely been the case, this is especially due to the intervention of business intelligence and how big it is. I've been in so many conferences and spoken on topics related to Performance Management and one of the key initiatives that are running in most organizations is business intelligence and how it's supposed to furnish Performance Management and add value to the organization.

In a nutshell, the answers are always there, however the adoption itself is, which could be on a different level from one organization to the other depending on the maturity level.

3. What are your thoughts on the relationship between Performance Management at organizational, departmental and individual level?

Performance Management is the framework; it's like the blood running in the veins of the organization. I'm not saying that it should sit within a certain function in isolation from the rest of the business, that would definitely kill it at the start. It has to be embedded in the organization, it has to be a centralized overview of what's going on at the organizational level, but as you cascade it down to the division and to

the individual level that sort of alignment has to always exist and in fact when I say Performance Management I would like to relate it very much to alignment across the organization and the functional level and at the individual level and alignment here is more than just a cascading of objectives into the organization, alignment is making sure that everyone is performing towards a certain goal, that's really the heart of Performance Management.

As I mentioned there is a centralized element and there is a decentralized element because it has to live in the blood and soul of the business, but it's definitely not an isolated function and it's definitely not something that should be left

> Realizing the benefit of the product is actually the heart of PM, whatever that is. Whether it's a service or a product or a project, whatever it is, realizing benefits is the heart of PM.

fragmented across the organization.

4. What are the 2012 key trends in Performance Management from the perspective of your knowledge and experience in this field?

There are several of them. There is a structural trend where PM now gets to be recognized as a core central function, or the central piece of it is now being recognized and in fact the supporting structure like the RSM or the corporate strategy office or

whatever you want to call it but at the end of the day now part of our business is PM even if you still call it quality, quality function. There is a trend moving towards from simply monitoring your performance laterally to improving your performance and realizing benefits, that's on the operational level and the project level, so in a sense if I was to explore it in one piece, on a project level, I mean if you look at the standard definition of a project, start to end, delivering a new product or service, I have a strong feeling you get a standard definition because you have been running so many projects across all the industries and all the places that I worked in as a consultant, at the end of the day they get a nice deliverable, especially for corporate development sort of projects, they recognize the implementation, they put it on the shelf but they never use it, and they never actually realize the benefit of that product. Realizing the benefit of the product is actually the heart of PM, whatever that is. Whether it's a service or a product or a project, whatever it is, realizing benefits is the heart of PM.

So moving from output delivery from a deliverable perspective towards benefits realization is another trend in PM.

5. What aspects of Performance Management should be explored more through research?

The question is not much different to the previous question, if I'm looking at trends, then obviously, those trends have to be reflected in research, especially in applied research and that's the part of research that I honor.

So the concept behind benefits realization is here in its early stages and I have evidence for that. The concept of benefits management has to mature and sit within the organization. The concept of Risk Management, there has been so many different talks on Risk Management and how to align the Risk Management with the Performance Management with the Strategic Management all of them into one framework, that's what David Norton and Robert Kaplan have been working on recently but again, I can see that there is always a confusion between enterprise risk management, project risk management the line is not clear and it should be the fact that there is even some research which suggests the establishment of offices that are looking at just enterprise risk management. Then we get into the dilemma of how many offices do we have to create so you don't want to spread yourself too thin. Therefore, I think that benefits realization is definitely a concept that has to be studied in future research, Risk Management and aligning that to Performance Management, change management, which is another key element and how does it relate back to Project Management because in the end they all relate back to Performance Management.

Change Management is a gear on its own that holds everything else to one. It's what I would call the heart and soul of the machine. One research that I'm working on with some of my colleagues is something called, "The Value Machine". "The Value Machine", if you would graph it, is basically five gears that are all working together in a machine structure. Performance Management is actually one of those gears, Change Management is another gear, Portfolio Management is another gear, Strategy Management and Knowledge Management. Each one of those elements has been studied thoroughly. But linking each of those elements together into one cohesive machine, as it runs it adds value to the organization is something that I haven't seen much of and something I haven't found much research on.

So from a larger perspective, linking all these elements together is definitely something that will add value from a micro-perspective on Performance Management, as I said, risk and benefits.

6. Please provide some examples of organizations which you would recommend for study due to their approach to Performance Management and achievements.

I would definitely look at the best companies in the world. There are so many different rankings from the best companies in the world. When you talk about PM, there are so many different approaches to them. We can look at Balanced Scorecard. Some people even consider Six Sigma as a PM tool. There are so many different approaches that have been ranked and have been studied in terms of their adoption in large organizations and what sort of value each of one of them presents and there

is a ranking for it and actually Balanced Scorecard would be number 1.

In terms of sectors, let me give you an example of the Abu Dhabi Government. It's one of the very few governments in the world that has an inspiring vision to become one of the top five governments in the world. They have established a real state-of-the-art PM framework that is based on the Balanced Scorecard. They have got the hall of fame work on and Norton and Kaplan in terms of PM framework. But all that aside, if you see things that are happening on the ground, it has nothing to do with the vision or the best framework that has been

> "The Value Machine", if you would graph it, is basically five gears that are all working together in a machine structure. Performance Management is actually one of those gears, Change Management is another gear, Portfolio Management is another gear, Strategy Management and Knowledge Management.

adopted. Why? Because of the culture here and that's the key element of the induction of Performance Management. The culture does not support it. They have different opinions, they have different management styles, because they still haven't aligned one single management style to the entire government and it's still different from one entity to the other. Their adoption of PM changes and obviously they're not getting the benefits from it. What I'm trying to say here is that you can have the best system in the world and get an award for it, however, when you see things on the ground, you will see that there is a huge disconnection. But again, top companies in the world are very much accomplished everywhere and I would assume by default that they have an approach to PM that needs to be studied.

7. Which are the main challenges of Performance Management in practice today?

Adoption of the framework, understanding which frameworks are adopted in the first place, the interventions between those like Balanced Scorecard, Six Sigma, the FQM, The Excellence Model, you see all these things, but you don't see how you can make use of all these things together

or how you would evaluate them and then determine which one is the best for you. So that's a challenge in its own and to decide upon which Performance Management standard to adopt. Another thing is the culture and how it supports Performance Management and leadership, as well as the contribution of those tools to the success of any Performance Management framework that has been adopted.

8. What do you think should be improved in the use of Performance Management tools and processes?

If you look at the history the evolution of PM, you can conclude that there has been plenty of improvement, when it comes to PM tools and processes. There is always room for improvement, but in terms of the maturity, in terms of tools, in terms of software, in terms of frameworks, there are plenty of them. I think the real issue is them is with the use and adoption. There are several works done on the design components of these tools so the use and the adoption has been researched and discussed in terms of improvement.

If you're talking about the actual use, I would talk about the behavioral side, not about the technical side. Some aspects especially when you get to the use stage, the behavioral side is actually more important than anything else. There needs to be some behavioral research done, to look at different kinds of organizations and see what attributes they need to have, in order for them to improve their adoption and use of PM tools. This is one of the things which is a major research element.

9. What would you consider best practice in Performance Management?

I'm very much more towards the Balanced Scorecard as a framework not just for Performance Management but for the entire cycle of strategy management. Referring to the latest execution premium process that was developed by Norton and Kaplan, I see that as one of the best practices in the market today. The latest version of the EFQM 2010 as an excellence model is considered best practice today especially if you plan to use a tool like the Balanced Scorecard you can get benefits from both without confusing people by giving the perception that you're using two different tools for Performance Management. These I would consider as best practices in terms of the design.

In terms of adoption, there is no best practice. But it is very important to make sure that there is some sort of a plan in place, to guarantee that top leadership will always be supporting, committed to these sorts of relationships or any sort of Performance Management or to any sort of corporate development project at all. And that's a lot easier said than done, but having a plan in place makes sure that that commitment is stable and consistent across the lifecycle of the project, from development to use to improvement and assistance of the tool itself. There is no such best practice for that other than making sure that you follow the process and that you are very sensitive to the cultural aspects and the behaviors of the people that you're dealing with.

A recent study that was conducted on PM adopted says it that 60% of these projects fail in general, if you're going to have the top leadership committed to it, you can increase the chances of success. You can barely survive at 60%, so just imagine if you don't have that sort of support, so how can we handle that? That makes it a very critical issue to be looked at. Compared to other sort of processes in general, of course, the general statement, the external stakeholders have to be satisfied otherwise it doesn't work, but I'm talking about specific stakeholders and I'm talking about a specific tool that relates to Performance Management, the alignment and the support, the commitment on an ongoing basis is key.

10. Which aspects of Performance Management should be emphasized during educational programs?

The behavioral aspect of adoption needs to be emphasized, the key success factors of how to adopt PM and what needs to be done to make sure you manage those success factors and that they're always there. That needs to be emphasized. You want to graduate practitioners as much as possible, that's the general problem across education in general. You definitely want to graduate practitioners in PM and there's no way that this can happen unless they are very much into reality.

Don't just rely on the fact that when they graduate, they will work and they will find out about these things themselves or they will learn it from something else. Teach them the theory from practice. A lot of graduates when they come out into the real world, they're preparing to balance and reduce the margin between the expectations and the real world expectations.

> The tools, the systems the processes they're all in the books, they're there. The major barrier that you will always have is that you need to be a very interactive, proactive person.

11. What are the barriers to achieving higher levels of proficiency in Performance Management among practitioners?

The more you do it, the more you get better at it. You also have to realize that yes, if you are working as a consultant, then yes you can do it in many places. If you do it as an internal consultant, then you get the benefit of seeing the whole cycle, not just the design elements of it but also the use of it, and also how the system is used.

So the barriers will definitely depend on the kind of job that you're doing. Generally speaking, I wouldn't see training, education and knowledge as a barrier because that is there, not only are you going to train in courses or something like that, but it's also in terms of self-development.

The thing with any Performance Management specialist or expert or consultant or whatever is that he needs to have very good communication skills. He needs to be able to communicate and communicate and communicate. He needs to be able to listen, he needs to have that soft side he needs to be patient, very patient and he needs to be able to create a dialogue. All the things that I am saying here are on the soft side, but that's what it is. The tools, the systems the processes they're all in the books, they're there. The major barrier that you will always have is that you need to be a very interactive, proactive person. We all know that there are so many people who say that you are born like this or not. I oppose that, I see that you can always develop that side of yourself, that soft side of yourself.

That's the key barrier that I see specifically for PM for professionals.

12. What Performance Management question would you like to have answered?

I would relate it back to the research question that I am currently working on here: how does Performance Management fit in the bigger picture? There are other players, there are other gears; the alignment of these has to be in place. There is no doubt that each one of those elements has their own value, but it's how you find the synergy between all those for even better value.

I understand that this study is very much focused on Performance Management but I also would definitely suggest that in the future, you or any other person who is interested in Performance Management research would need to analyse the bigger picture and how Performance Management fits into the bigger picture. That's the one thing that I would say would be a very beneficial exercise.

13. Which were the recent achievements in generating value from Performance Management in your organization?

It's a long-term process, I can not say that the organization has finished with its achievements, even though the PM team is convinced that the decisions and the strategy have been cascaded down to the individual level. They all now know what the strategy is all about, but there was a huge lapse in terms of the awareness amongst entities in the organization. All these things happen but in terms of the adoption and the use this is now the time that we are looking at that and I can tell you now that we had many challenges, especially since we had a recent change in management. Different management styles are key to handling and you always have to present the case for PM and the value of it and that is not just for PM. It's for the whole strategy management framework. So there are achievements in terms of designing, but in terms of the use and the adoption, they are in the process of doing that. ∎

Interviewee name:
Mabrouk Aib
Title:
Chief Performance Officer
Organization:
HydraPharm Group
Country:
Algeria
Continent:
Africa

second one is that of the people who think strategy emerges from the organization step by step. You have to make sure these two perspectives fit into the company's reality.

It's easy from the first point of view or from the elaborated strategy point of view. It's easy to build metrics and Performance Management systems but from the second point of view it's not that easy because you do not have the clear idea about what the strategy is and how to describe the strategic objectives to the organization. Therefore, I think that those two things are key trends.

1. What does the term Performance Management mean to you?

It's a way to put in place a system that enables strategy execution. It's about aligning organizational strategy and aligning people to strategic objectives. It is a two-way process. It is top-down and bottom-up. If your system doesn't tell employees what to do, they won't understand the objectives and be able to link it back to the overall strategy. It is also important to give feedback to top level managers and to talk to the managers so that they can apply the strategy to the frontline.

2. What drives interest in Performance Management?

There are two points:
- It's how the system can be put into the organization. The mainstream habit is to use Balanced Scorecards but how you can implement this in your own given the structure of the organization, the structure of the company, the people and the skills you refer to?
- The second part is about information systems and this is a local problem, as well as an issue all over the world. In Algeria, we have a lot to do regarding the improvement of information systems. If you want Performance Management Systems to work correctly, you need to have the correct information. The issue is to be able to fit Performance Management Systems within a company that does not have a very efficient information system. Maybe the question that should be answered first is: "Do you have an information system?". Only after this you can try and put in place a Performance Management System.

3. What are your thoughts on the relationship between Performance Management at organizational, departmental and individual level?

It is a question of process between the different departments of the oorganization. Thus, you have the question of performance measurement systems and we link that to variable salaries for individuals. There is a strong relationship between PM at an individual level going to upper level and going between employees at a departmental level, because usually you do not grant variable salary to an individual without taking into consideration the department level of the individual. You should always put in the variable part of the salary and you should put more emphasis on the success and behavior of the employee.

4. What are the 2012 key trends in Performance Management from the perspective of your knowledge and experience in this field?

From my point of view, trends will be PM strategy. People will be interested in the way strategy is elaborated within the

organization. This is what we call strategy in practice. You have to make current strategy research and take into account at least two perspectives. One is the corporate planning and consultants' perspective - those think that strategy is mainly planned and elaborated in a structured manner. The

Performance Management is a way to put in place a system that enables strategy execution. It's about aligning organizational strategy and aligning people to strategic objectives.

5. What aspects of Performance Management should be explored more through research?

I think it would be interesting to see the link between Performance Management and the culture of the organization. It is something that is difficult for practitioners to give answers to. I think that relationship is interesting and there should be more light shed on this issue.

6. Please provide some examples of organizations which you would recommend for study due to their approach to Performance Management and achievements.

There is a PM system in our company, so it is very interesting to do such work and actually, that's what I'm doing. Our co-operation with École Nationale Polytehnique allows us to put in place a reverse transfer, in order to get people from abroad. I think that is a very good case to study.

7. Which are the main challenges of Performance Management in practice today?

It's about being able to have a formal strategy. I've been discussing with colleagues from different companies and usually a company has a strategy, but it largely remains in the upper management, with the founder of the company or with the CEO. But what is formally expressed is sometimes different. It could be different from the strategy or only part of the strategy because it's not easy to formalize. It may only seem clear to certain people, but that's not always the case. In a lot of companies at the top management level, people do have a good idea as to where they are going to be in the future, but not a clear and concise idea. So it's a difficult process taking this general idea of a strategic objective and forming metrics. I think this is one of the main challenges. The second challenge is about information systems, which I discussed earlier.

8. What do you think should be improved in the use of Performance Management tools and processes?

Companies I know use spreadsheets like Excel. Some of them are using information from their ERP and they have large databases but in the end, a lot of them just use a spreadsheet. I think they should use more specific tools.

9. What would you consider best practice in Performance Management?

There are so many company cultures, but from my point of view, it is important to have a Performance Management taskforce or commission. It's not a permanent structure, but it's a structure with the high level people who meet regularly and assess the Performance Management system, something like a steering committee. The Performance Management system becomes a project in the company and is something that you have to improve. The steering committee is formed by executives from top management, from different departments, like finance and HR. Performance Management is through all the organization

> If you want Performance Management Systems to work correctly, you need to have the correct information. The issue is to be able to fit Performance Management Systems within a company that does not have a very efficient information system.

and all the departments and functions and it's important to have sponsoring from the top of the company.

10. Which aspects of Performance Management should be emphasized during educational programs?

You have to know how all those processes within the company are linked and the interrelations between the processes, because if you do not understand this, you can not know what Performance Management is for. You will learn about finance, you will learn about HR, you will learn about marketing but you do not have a clear idea about the link between all those processes and functions in the company, how a company works globally. In particular, the interfaces between all those functions and perimeters. Usually people in marketing do not understand what's going on outside and the same with finance, etc.

The second point is that employees are a main part of Performance Management. At the end of the day, the performance is run by all those guys within the system, they need to understand how it works because the link between how an employee reacts and the Performance Management system is important. It's not at all just because they are part of the system. It's not easy to understand how to give the right incentive. To be sure, that's why we're aligning people to our strategy objectives. You have to understand how people are, how it works. You can also relate this point to the question about what should be covered more in research. For example, what is motivation and the link with Performance Management. ▨

Interviewee name:
Peter Ndaa
Title:
CEO
Organization:
Balanced Scorecard Eastern Africa
Country:
Kenya
Continent:
Africa

1. What does the term Performance Management mean to you?

It's the management of the execution of a portfolio of strategic initiatives (projects and action plans), monitoring progress towards desired strategic results and taking corrective actions, where necessary, to ensure the accomplishment of the desired results.

2. What drives interest in Performance Management?

The need to increase institutional or organization productivity drives interest in Performance Management.

3. What are your thoughts on the relationship between Performance Management at organizational, departmental and individual level?

Organizational performance is an aggregation of the performance of its departments. The performance of departments is an aggregation of the performance of the individuals within that department. Where there is no action, there is no result. Projects and action plans are executed by individuals located in different parts of organization. Unless the individuals complete their tasks in full, on time and deliver results, then an organization will not perform.

4. What are the 2012 key trends in Performance Management from the perspective of your knowledge and experience in this field?

An integrated approach to Performance Management that enables the linking of the dots between strategic performance and individual performance is a key trend. To this end, there has been an increase in the adoption of the Balanced Scorecard strategic planning and management system in Africa. Several governments e.g. Kenya, Uganda, Ethiopia have declared this as the preferred Performance Management system for public sector.

5. What aspects of Performance Management should be explored more through research?
- The effect of Performance Management system on individuals within the organization
- Success stories in both the private and public sector.

6. Please provide some examples of organizations which you would recommend for study due to their approach to Performance Management and achievements.
- Kenya Red Cross
- Volta River Authority (Ghana)
- Uganda Revenue Authority
- The Bank of Uganda
- Kenya Electricity Generation Company
- The Government of the Republic of Botswana
- The Ministry of Health, The Federal Republic of Ethiopia

7. Which are the main challenges of Performance Management in practice today?
- Leadership commitment
- Organizational Culture
- Competencies, especially consultants' knowledge.

8. What do you think should be improved in the use of Performance Management tools and processes?
- Communication and change management should be entrenched in the processes
- Management of projects portofolio.

> Organizational performance is an aggregation of the performance of its departments. The performance of departments is an aggregation of the performance of the individuals within that department. Where there is no action, there is no result.

9. What would you consider best practice in Performance Management?
- Engaged leadership
- Agree on a single set of terminology
- Communicate with more than just the "special few"
- Think of this as a marathon – not just a sprint
- Avoid the "Rush to judgments": performance measures, our current projects, software
- Reward desired behavior changes

- Plan for and manage change
- Follow through – don't lose momentum.

10. Which aspects of Performance Management should be emphasized during educational programs?
- Leadership
- Communication and Change Management
- Developing objectives at the right strategic altitude
- Performance measurement and target setting
- Project Management.

11. What are the barriers to achieving higher levels of proficiency in Performance Management among practitioners?
- Competency

12. As a consultant, what are the most common issues that your customers raised related to Performance Management?
The most common questions are:
- How to hold individuals at all levels of the organization accountable?
- How to manage change in order to adopt a performance culture in an organization?
- How to "buy – in'" employees?

Interviewee name:
Alan Meekings
Title:
Founding Director
Organization:
Landmark Consulting
Country:
UK
Continent:
Europe

1. What does the term Performance Management mean to you?

The term Performance Management can be confusing. For instance, when Human Resource professionals use this term, they are often thinking about the performance of individual members of staff and topics such as individual appraisal and reward and recognition, rather than collective organizational performance.

To differentiate between individual Performance Management and collective organizational Performance Management, the term Performance Measurement and Management is widely used, especially in academia.

While this phrase goes some way to reducing the confusion between individual Performance Management and collective Performance Management, there are some downsides to using this term, not only because adding the word 'measurement' can lead organizations to overly focus on the design and implementation of metrics, but also because of the seek to get the maximum value out of the use of performance information, for instance to make better decisions faster.

Hence, I prefer the term Organizational Performance Management instead. To me, this emcompasses all the dimensions of organizational performance, such as strategy development and execution, operational excellence and continual improvement, as well as individual performance and development.

To me, what seems to be important though, is distinguishing between improving the way the work gets done in organizations, commonly referred to as "process improvement" and improving the way organisations are managed, which could be described as "management process improvement".

2. What drives interest in Performance Management?

In the public sector in the UK, at least over the past decade or so, the focus has been seeking to improve outcomes and the beneficial impact of public services. This has caused significant attention to be paid to organizational Performance Management across the whole public sector in the UK.

However, while the election of the Labour Government in 1997 focused its attention on the issue of organizational Performance Management, it also gave free rein to arbitrary numerical target-setting at an unprecedented scale. Dr. Deming would have been appalled. Sadly, the legacy of this flawed approach to improve organizational performance is still evident today, even 15 years later.

In the commercial sector in the UK, recent financial crises and the current recession have reminded organizations of Dr. Deming's famous adage, that "survival is not compulsory" on a competitive market. Unfortunately, this situation tended to encourage organizations to scale back on their aspirations for fundamental improvement, in favour of surviving as best as they can. The message that deliberately improves the way organizations are managed pays for itself within weeks, even if is difficult to put across at the moment.

3. What are your thoughts on the relationship between Performance Management at organizational, departmental and individual level?

My answer to this important question is to stress the importance of developing an explicit, rigorously defined "Performance Architecture", which offers answers to two key questions: (a) who needs to look at what performance information, why, when and how; and (b) how differing functions and levels of management should best integrate and inter-relate.

These two headline questions also invite attention to a series of subsidiary issues, such as: how are individuals and teams best enabled to explore their own relevant performance information, how to identify actionable insights and track the impact of decisions and actions they take; how is performance planning going to be brought to life in practice; and how is a vibrant

> To me, what seems to be important, though, is distinguishing between improving the way the work gets done in organizations, commonly referred to as "process improvement" and improving the way organizations are managed, which could be described as "management process improvement".

performance culture best implemented and sustained.

It is important to start by thinking about how performance information needs to be used in practice (by whom, why, when and how and between functions and managerial levels), rather than about how performance metrics should be put in place.

Given this approach, performance metrics become self-correcting, in the sense that any metrics that prove unhelpful will be discarded and any new metrics required will be embraced and actively used.

This encapsulates the difference between pushing performance metrics on an organization and having performance metrics pulled through by demand. The difference is profound.

In short, my answer to your question about "Performance Management at organizational, departmental and individual level" is to design a performance architecture that specifically answers this question.

4. What are the 2012 key trends in Performance Management from the perspective of your knowledge and experience in this field?

Stepping back and reflecting on the papers I have read in the Performance Management field, over the last 25 years, I have to say they are mostly about frameworks and metrics, rather than about the use of performance information in practice, let alone about how to create a vibrant, sustainable performance culture.

Also, I see attention within the academic community being focused on subsidiary topics, such as Risk Management. Obviously, Risk Management is an interesting and important topic in its own right, but it palls into insignificance, in comparison with the broader opportunity to improve the way organizations are managed.

In this context, I see widespread disconnectedness and waste in the way organizations are managed.

Indeed, as a management consultant, I constantly come across examples of disconnectedness, such as: executive directors not behaving as a real team (instead, they are pursuing various functional priorities and personal incentives); strategy formulation and execution disconnected from day-to-day operational delivery and pressures to meet the annual budget; functions and managerial levels disconnected from each other (with no mechanism for surfacing or addressing issues appropriately, from frontline to boardroom); decisions and actions being avoided, countermanded or endlessly revisited, up, down and across the organisation; a high level of routine in management reports, seen as costly to prepare and largely disconnected from the key issues and opportunities that most influence organizational performance, improvement and adaptability; the people best placed to drive performance and innovation, disconnected from: (a) actionable insights into levers - if they could pull that, it would actually make a real difference; and (b) the essential feedback needed to show the impact of decisions and actions taken; and performance being seen primarily as an attribute of individual competence and motivation, assessed through an individual performance appraisal process, implemented hierarchically, rather than based on the outcome of effective leadership, management decision-making and teamwork, coupled with rigorous efforts to improve the system in which individuals are required to work.

My answer to such widespread disconnectedness is the approach I call "Connected Performance". This encompasses five elements, namely: Performance Architecture, Performance

Exploration, Performance Planning, Performance Culture and Successful Implementation.

I've already mentioned the idea of

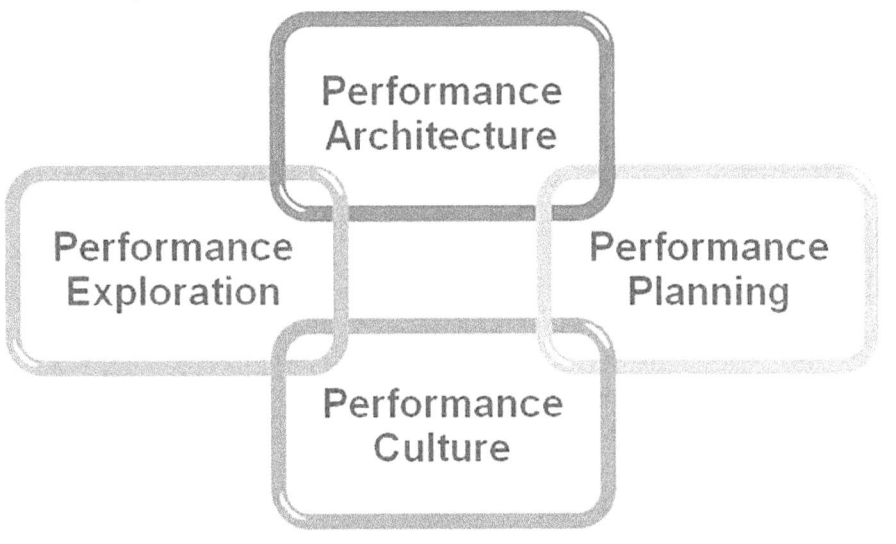

developing an appropriate Performance Architecture. However, there is no point in having even the most elegant Performance Architecture, unless the other four essential elements of Connected Performance are not well-developed too. This is something my colleagues and I will be addressing in our paper for this year's biennial PMA conference in Cambridge, in July.

Incidentally, it is also worth mentioning that, under the heading of Performance Exploration, Professor Tom Davenport's phrase - "Competing on Analytics" is relevant. As Professor Davenport explains, organizations with a lot of fast-moving operational data now have a real opportunity to move from "drowning in their data" to "competing on analytics". Unfortunately, few organizations worldwide currently exhibit the highest maturity level of "Competing on Analytics" that Professor Davenport describes. However, interest in this field seems to be growing exponentially. This is great news, as it may encourage organizations to think more rigorously about how to enable frontline staff and managers at all levels to extract actionable insights from their data, at the speed of thought (rather than having to submit queries to a central analytical team).

5. What aspects of Performance Management should be explored more through research?

I see the next big opportunity for research in the Performance Management field as focusing on ways to improve the way organizations are managed, rather than on improving how their work gets done, either internally and/or across end-to-end supply chains.

This could help move the thinking forward from pedestrian, well-understood topics, such as strategy development and execution, the definition of metrics and so on to something more exciting and potentially helpful.

> It is important to start by thinking about how performance information needs to be used in practice (by whom, why, when and how and between functions and managerial levels), rather than about how performance metrics should be put in place.

6. Please provide some examples of organizations which you would recommend for study due to their approach to Performance Management and achievements.

While I'm happy to talk you privately through three examples of leading-edge work my colleagues and I have recently

done in this field, I wouldn't wish these examples to be quoted publicly without specific permission from my clients.

7. Which are the main challenges of Performance Management in practice today?

Over the years, I've developed a fishbone diagram, outlining common root causes behind the failure of initiatives in the field of Performance Measurement and Management to deliver to their full potential.

You could group these several causes of failure into four generic areas: (1) Motivation - why would organizations wish to improve the way they are managed?; (2) Mobilization and Communication - how best to explain to people how to get involved and incorporate their thinking and suggestions?; (3) Design and Implementation - what best to do and how best to do it?; and (4) Support and Coaching - how to address individual and collective fears? What's important, of course, is to look at these typical causes of failure and deliberately address them. The answer is not to worry about strategic management frameworks, performance metric definition, target-setting et al, but instead to think deeply about how performance information should be used by whom, why, when and how, along with issues around implementation.

8. What do you think should be improved in the use of Performance Management tools and processes?

A greater awareness of the framework which I call "Connected Performance".

9. What would you consider best practice in Performance Management?

I think my answer to this question is the same as my answer to your earlier question, that's to say Connected Performance.

10. Which aspects of Performance Management should be emphasized during educational programs?

I think the most important thing to communicate to students is the importance of starting with the use of performance information, rather than with defining what needs to be measured.

At the risk of sounding like a broken record, this includes addressing questions such as: (a) who needs to look at what performance information, why, when and how; and (b) how differing functions and levels of management should best integrate and inter-relate.

11. What are the barriers to achieving higher levels of proficiency in Performance Management among practitioners?

I think the biggest barrier to moving the thinking forward in the field of Performance Management is enabling people who work in academia to appreciate the art of the possible in this field and what good really looks like. Academics have a vital role in understanding and communicating best practice.

However, it's obviously not their fault if they don't really understand what best practice looks like. How could they possibly know, if they have no access to leading practice, especially on a historic basis?

Hence, I suggest that when practitioners embark on interesting engagements in this field, it would be helpful if there was some way to signal to people in academia the opportunity to track either a specific initiative or a longer-term timeline.

12. What Performance Management

I see the next big opportunity for research in the Performance Management field as focusing on ways to improve the way organizations are managed, rather than on improving how their work gets done, either internally and/or across end-to-end supply chains.

question would you like to have answered?

I think I would like to have recognized the fact that the most important question now, in terms of improving organizational performance, is how to improve the way organizations are managed, rather than improving the way their work gets done.

While it's great that many people have "learned to see" muda, mura and muri as waste in operational processes, I think the time has come for us to "learn to see" muda, mura and muri as waste in management processes too.

13. As a consultant, what are the most common issues that your customers raised related to Performance Management?

Two presenting issues typically occur. Clients recognise that they are either: (a) drowning in their data and sense they may not necessarily be measuring or responding to the right things; or (b) have read about "Competing on Analytics" or have software providers pestering them to buy new analytical tools, enterprise-wide software.

Typically clients don't immediately understand the potential benefits of improving how their organisations are managed. ▓

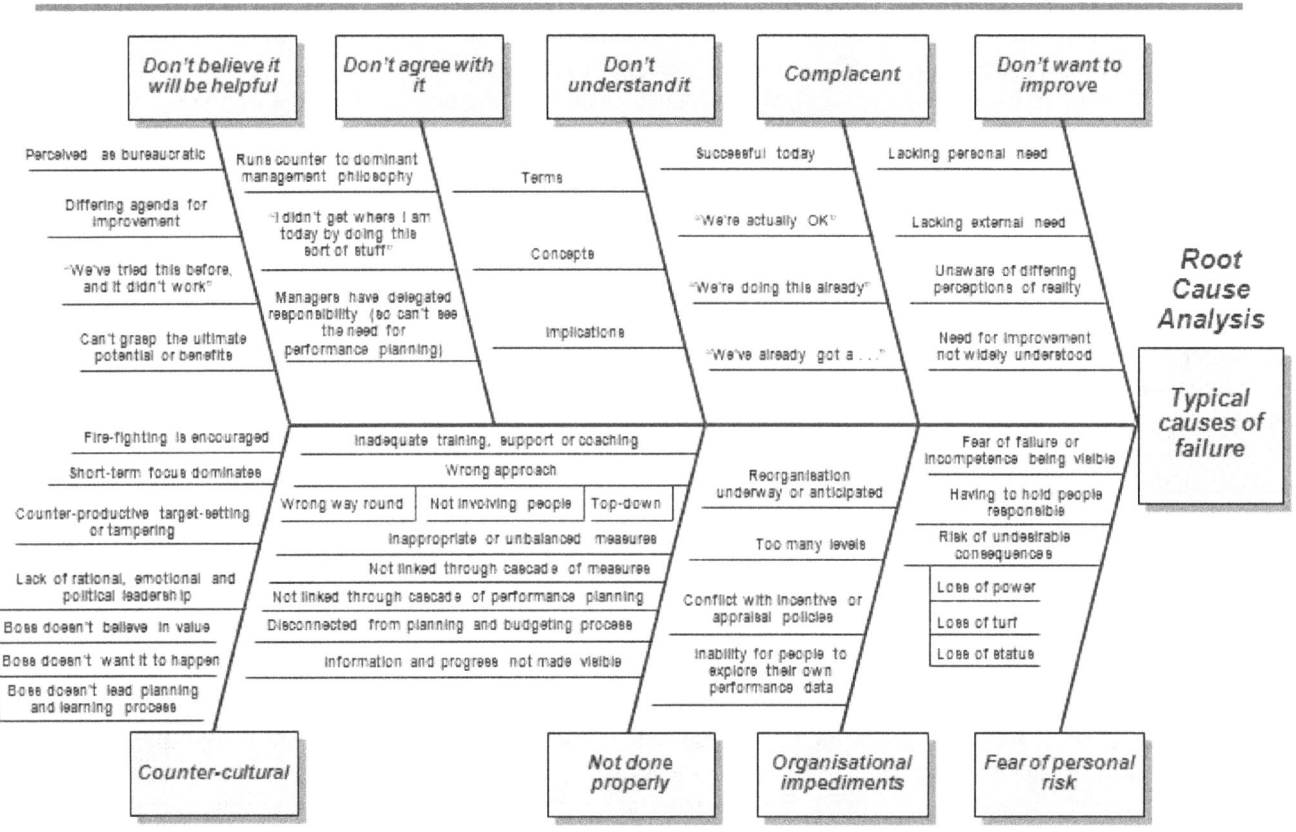

Why do performance measurement and management initiatives often fail to deliver their full potential benefits?

Interviewee name:
Jodi Traversaro with the support of the California Performance Management Council
Title:
Learning and Performance Management Manager
Organization:
California Department of Personnel Administration
Country:
USA
Continent:
North America

1. What does the term Performance Management mean to you?

The critically interconnected management processes that work together to enable an organization to achieve results. Performance Management includes key practices to ensure organizations set priorities and operational plans, establish targets and relevant metrics, and create mechanisms to analyze, evaluate and report progress at regular intervals. It also includes activities to make necessary adjustments and improvements to ensure that the organization remains pointed in a direction that supports its mission and achieve its results in the most effective and efficient manner. (Note: as defined in Performance Management in California State Government, An advisory report from the Performance Management Council, 2010).

2. What drives interest in Performance Management?

The general goal to make government operations more effective and efficient drives interest in this field within the public service. Federal Government grants require it, the economic decline, which is growing public interest on how well the Government is performing with tax dollars (what are they getting for what they are paying), the need to use performance measures to evaluate program effectiveness, as well as to use data to drive program efficiencies. The press, such as newspapers is another driver.

3. What are your thoughts on the relationship between Performance Management at organizational, departmental and individual level?

Performance Management is a tool used sporadically throughout State Government, more so in some agencies and departments than others. Ideally, performance measures should track strategic goals in the broadest sense throughout all levels, but also be used in more detailed form to drill down into work (to help managers manage and leaders lead). The program metric is also the employee metric, it should help

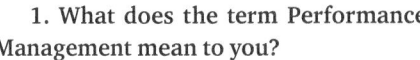

> In an ideal world, everybody would have something like a baseball card where you can see statistic and how they contribute to the team. So I believe that individual statistics contribute to organization or team performance, which can contribute to the department or state-wide performance. But we need to make sure that the metrics we use are the right metrics or they can be applied in an appropriate way.

managers manage and help leaders lead. So you would have individual performance that is tied to term performance, program performance, organizational performance and of course overall performance.

But one thing to note is that in the State Government of California, we have a unique situation, generated by the unionized workers. By and large, here in California, I can not tell a police officer that he must write 50 tickets per hour. There are multiple rules that prohibit governments to set employee performance metrics for various reasons. In the Government, we refer to those metrics as "performance standards". So in fact the reality of public work is we have to create metrics that achieve results without compromising the fairness of what we do.

In an ideal world, everybody would have something like a baseball card where you can see the statistic and how they contribute to the team. So I believe that individual statistics can contribute to organization or team performance, which can contribute to the department or statewide performance. But we need to make sure that the metrics we use are the right metrics or they can be applied in an appropriate way.

4. What are the 2012 key trends in Performance Management from the perspective of your knowledge and experience in this field?

Well, I think one of the key trends is really applying Performance Management in the Government. Oftentimes, we have the private sector measuring its bottom line – revenue. In Government operations you have an even more unique challenge in trying to measure the value of public service. So I think the key trends will be to do a better job at measuring the value of Government services. From that you will find the efficiency of the Government.

Another trend is evaluating what people would call the "immeasurable", for example, the value of the life of a duck, or the value of a state park. So, I think there is the measurement challenge in Government that will be overcome and, because of the tremendous loads of data in the Internet, we will do a much better job connecting dots as data will be matched up now, when before it was never matched up. So I see automation, connecting dots, data-driving decision-making and the desire for transparency in Government as huge trends that would force us to do things differently in the Government.

In addition, I think our network is better

than it ever was in connecting talents and experts in the field to people who need to know. So because of that, I think the scale of the people in this field is rapidly increasing. It just has such a movement to make data-driven decisions. And the need of data to make the decisions in Performance Management is driving us to measure and automate that in the network and then make it transparent. Automation, networking, transparency, collaboration are all part of the tremendous demand for our public to be more efficient.

5. What aspects of Performance Management should be explored more through research?

There are several aspects including: how to teach people about the benefits; how to get people to adopt Performance Management in the management practices (how to get started is very hard); how to build the culture that accepts measurements and is adaptable to changing them. So I think there is a general fear of data and I think there is also a fear of measuring people's performance with metrics.

So as you know, we've got this massive trend in the US-the baby boom issue. The baby boomers from the World War II are going to retire and are replaced by young people who are demanding a flexible working environment and want to be evaluated on results, not on whether they show up at work. So in California, and in the US, we have a real shift in work preferences and what happens is the younger generation would like to be measured on their contributions to the organization. But our current Performance Management systems are primarily focusing on the program at the departmental level, and not on the individual level.

The question will be how we can get unions to buy into result-oriented work? And I think what happens the Government is that people are measured on whether or not they can arrive to work on time, instead of whether or not they did a great job on writing something on saving the State ten million dollars. In the private sector you can reference based on sales. You can see how much revenue one individual generates. In Government we don't generate sales.

We serve the public, so how we measure performance is very different. We have to measure how much money we save. To take a step further, there is a trend for people to say that. In fact there is a book called "Government Just Doesn't Make Widgets". So there are many books that help the Government try and measure its value or

> Here in California, I can not tell a police officer that he must write 50 tickets per hour. There are multiple rules that prohibit governments for setting employee performance metrics for various reasons. In government, we refer to those metrics as "performance standards". So in fact the reality of public work is we have to create metrics that achieve results without compromising the fairness of what we do.

its work. All I'm trying to say is that there is an area of research that is needed on how we can get the labor organizations to buy it, to adopt Performance Management for employees because sometimes managers focus on things that are not as important as the results. And so a trend of management is to create a more result-oriented work environment. And often times the new generations would like flexible schedules and they want to know what they need to get done and until when and they will get it done in their own way, on their own time.

So what we have in the Government, here in California, is a style of management that does not match the preferences of our younger generation. Meanwhile we have this trend of Performance Management that is very strong in California and started at the federal level in 1996, but it has come out repeatedly and we have failed to implement it. Two weeks ago, our Governor sent an executive order that requires every State department to build Performance Management. Therefore, there is a lot of interest here because the Government said we need to do this. But we see challenges when it gets to the individual level.

6. Please provide some examples of organizations which you would recommend for study due to their approach to Performance Management and achievements.

Well, of course, I'm going to focus on Government. So I think the Federal Government is incredible. The US Federal Government has done an incredible job. And our President has actually just passed the new law that requires even more work to be done in this area.

For the State of California, there have been great efforts in our Tax Revenue Department, our income tax department called the Franchise Tax Board and we also have had some great achievements through our present system. We have 60,000 people that work in our Department of Corrections and Rehabilitation. That's a department which runs all the State prisons. Also we had a large effort put into our Business Transportation and Housing Agency and into their work with the Highway Patrol and also into our Department of Moto Vehicle and the Transportation Agency that handles our roads and bridges and the major highways. So there is a great effort in another large area there.

The State of Virginia is another quite good example. They have Balanced Scorecards for a lot of departments and agencies. Within them, they have a HR Agency. This Agency has defined various goals and objectives and it will tell you where they are with each of them and it's very exciting that you can drill down and see how everything is aligned with the goals. And that means people, programs and metrics are all very well done. And the Federal Government does the same thing. They have a department called Office Personnel Management (OPM) who oversees the employee Performance Management and has the whole system on aligning all employees with federal performance.

7. Which are the main challenges of Performance Management in practice today?

One of the main challenges is to teach leaders in Government what Performance Management is, what Performance Management looks like, how to implement Performance Management for all branches of the Government. We teach people all about Performance Management, how to do it, what it looks like and how we can all be rowing in the same direction. That is a huge effort. The challenge is, of course, getting started as we are sort of starting again. And of course we don't have a lot of money because we still are in a budget crisis so we need to do this with strong leadership and a willingness to invest in change.

Another issue is overcoming the fear of making your operations transparent. Your process is transparent; your program is transparent to greater scrutiny from outside parties. So you can imagine if everything I purchased for my program was made visible and somebody says you can buy that cheaper, I would be embarrassed. We do what we can with what we have and often times by making our decisions visible you open that up for public scrutiny and that can be scary.

Another challenge in the Government is how to measure our performance. How do you measure the performance of a park? How do you measure the economic impact of too many visitors? Or the environmental impact of global warming. In a nutshell, you have a whole host of challenges in Government Performance Management as opposed to private sectors.

8. What do you think should be improved in the use of Performance Management tools and processes?

Well, I wish we can collaborate more. I wish, for instance, which I know is completely possible, I could simply connect with all HRs. For example, imagine if all universities would have performance metrics tracking their activity, such as *what would be good performance regarding the cost of the school, how many people they let in, how many people graduate*. All universities would be connected, they would share their performance metrics and they could all compare their performance on a broad scale and then connect that up online and automate that. That's what I would like to see. I wish there was an automation connecting dots, getting everybody evaluated on similar metrics. So we, as customers, can see and make decisions. And leaders can make decisions.

9. What would you consider best practice in Performance Management?

I think I listed organizations recommend

for study in question 6. I think they have best practices in Performance Management. The other thing I mentioned sports teams' statistics. I use them as an example during my presentations. Kids can go to a candy store and buy a pack of trading cards,.., team sports cards... I usually buy 25 packs of cards and distribute them, and we have

> One of the key trends is really applying Performance Management in the Government. Oftentimes, we have the private sector measuring their bottom line – revenue. In government operations you have a more unique challenge in trying to measure the value of public service.

a worksheet on the back which has all those statistics. The front contains a picture of the player and the back contains their statistics, such as batting average, how many RBIs etc. What I love is that this shows people best practice: every team member and what the statistics are. There are really two primary reasons why I like this approach. First is the great illustration, as you know where you recognize talents. I love this part. I also love it because it has statistics that people would not normally come up with on their own, so that may become something like where I may think that is a bad statistic but it contributes to the overall team performance. For example, somebody in a baseball team that hits the ball but gets out may think that getting out is bad but what if the runner at third base came in?

When it comes to good practices, the sports teams are amazing and of course the government practices, such as the federal government is phenomenal.

(So are there any unsuccessful examples?)

The State of California tried implementing Performance Management systems in the 90s and failed. Between the years 1996-1998, the Federal Government had something called the Government Performance Result Art, (GPRA), which is a Government performance results pack. Then the state of California passed a similar law that was just like that. But instead of continuously implementing Performance Management, the State stopped. California passed a law, then stopped. There are lots of reasons why laws are passed and then not applied. I think we had several economic

issues. Passing legislation is a great idea but it takes a lot to implement because of the change management, the people, the data and the automation. We also had several different governors, that was about 20 years ago. So you had different leaders and different priorities.

I apologize for saying the State of California would be an example of a large entity that didn't implement Performance Management systems. Actually there have been varied departments which tried, but we want to do it statewide. We are a huge entity and there are some departments that have implemented great Performance Management within the State, as I listed them. The Tax Agencies and the Presidents are also parts of business. But those are just one group of California; the law said everybody would do it. So there have been some success stories in the State and now our Governor said we also need to do this.

10. Which aspects of Performance Management should be emphasized during educational programs?

I think it should be how to measure normally immeasurable things. I When I was an economic major, they would ask us how to measure happiness. So we came up with a measurement called "utils". For example, when I eat an ice-cream I have 5 utils. And then we would use that to describe the lots of diminishing returns, such as the first bite you give 5 utils and the second bite is 4. So, people need to think differently when you measure things that are not naturally easy to measure. They need to be taught how to create metrics to measure things normally considered immeasurable. The other things are people, Change Management, getting people to not fear the data. Getting people to lead and invest and initiate change. Teaching the people who attended educational programs on Performance Management to understand what performance looks like, for the organizations, for the program and for the individual, in order to be able to sell it to other leaders, because they can't do it by themselves.

Change management, Performance Management, Economics, networking in Sales, Marketing, and Industrial Psychology should be emphasized during educational programs.

Some other subjects, such as Accounting and IT are essential too. The reason I raise Accounting is accountants love metrics and data and our Tax Agencies are doing a great job.

It's very hard for people to understand that data can be measured. So I often use the example of a judge. Say there is a big oil spill, and the oil company has to be charged an amount that they have to pay. So every day in court systems across the world, judges are having to figure out what price the companies have to pay when they do something bad or wrong that impacts the environment. So there are people who specialized in figuring out what the impact is to the environment or on the cost of what they've done. If I like to use that as an example it is because this is not a completely foreign concept, we can measure the impact for instance, on rehabilitating a prisoner, or we can measure the impact of, for example, tax collection. If we have a business in California that is constantly late and in trouble and it takes all these people to try and get them to pay their taxes. Imagine if I educate them and then they become compliant for the rest of their business life. Then I can measure the reduction in cost through my time in educating business owners.

You can have law enforcement at a cost of $50,000-$100,000 to have a CHP officer on the highway sitting there all day, every day. But what happens is everybody slows down when they see him and we save lives. In Government operations, people have a hard time thinking how things can be measured or valued. Therefore, in the Government, we are measuring our reduction in loss of life, our dollars, our reduction in cost, our reduction on the environment and reduction of property. We have different metrics in the Government than we do in the private sector, we are almost non-profit. So you have to look at the Government and non-profits together, as opposed to the private sector. But I think we need to be held accountable, similar to the private sector, in delivering services. So customer satisfaction is important. But you know it is a very difficult task, so first you have to teach people to be successful in it. I think you would have to believe in it, both in the private sector and in the Government.

11. What are the barriers to achieving higher levels of proficiency in Performance Management among practitioners?

I don't think that in California we have dedicated professionals who are solely practitioners in Performance Management. Some of the barriers have to do with recognizing that it is separate, distinct function that people need training in, as they would be internal consultants. So in California, we typically match. Like me, I oversee the state of the training program for the employees and in addition they ask me to do the employee Performance Management. So then I reached out to the Performance Management Council and their jobs are primarily organizational or departmental performance. And their challenges, since they are usually strategic planning managers in Government Performance Management, they are typically added to a strategic planning manager's job because they need to develop a plan with metrics. And often times they are not able to get to the details where the metrics are built in or the key performance indicators are not built in to their plan. So in California, a lot of barriers have to do with, first of all, identifying the Key Performance

> Everything I do in state-wide training has elements to change the culture, to help leaders align their employees with the organizational metrics. In a sense, we are trying to raise awareness and move the Government with a very small group of passionate people.

Indicators or metrics. And the other issue is making sure we have got dedicated people to do this and that they are trained. And of course, as I mentioned earlier, we got unions. So for employees to be measured on their performance, we have to negotiate that with the unions. So there is a whole host of barriers to achieving a higher level in result of investing time and money which we just don't have.

12. What Performance Management question would you like to have answered?

N/A

Practitioner
Which were the recent achievements in generating value from Performance Management in your organization?

I would say a great achievement was the Governor putting an executive order out. Of course there were many achievements in the past ten years and some of them have great impacts. But now we have a statewide order to do a better job in this area. In my organization, what I'm very proud of is the Performance Management Council. Why I like this Council is because it has leaders in many departments across the State who come together, collaborate, share and try to make an important visible movement in the State Government. So sometimes they do this on their own time, but in the Government we are so big and this is the first time I have seen a group of amazing leaders come together once a month, share knowledge and take what they have learnt and apply it back in their organizations.

Another thing is, because I do state wide training, I was able to ask a leader of the Performance Management Council to give a statewide webinar on how to do it. And so, because of that, I was able to reach many, as I was able to train thousands of people. Because we have a partnership between the Performance Management Council and statewide training, I'm able to expand the knowledge very cheaply. In addition I was able to build in organizational performance into every employee performance training program. So I'm doing what I can from my role to really force the alignment between employee and organizational performance. I just wrote down a Performance Management resource guide and I think it was just two weeks ago that I released a website on Performance Management. I have got the Performance Management Council and I have got leaders willing to share knowledge. We have put out a big white paper and we help and work with the Governor's Office to get the executive order out. Everything I do in statewide training has elements to change the culture, to help leaders align their employees with the organizational metrics. In a sense, we are trying to raise awareness and move the Government with a very small group of passionate people. And I'm very proud of being part of that group; although there is so much more to be done. ∎

Interviewee name:
Kenneth Merchant
Title:
Deloitte & Touche LLP Chair of Accountancy
Organization:
University of Southern California
Country:
USA
Continent:
North America

1. What does the term Performance Management mean to you?

It's a broad term. I would include anything that is done to bring about the desired performance.

2. What drives interest in Performance Management?

I am not sure there is a lot of interest in Performance Management, per se. I don't see that term used a lot. But there is a continuing interest in many of the topics that would be included under the Performance Management rubric, and interest in some of them (e.g., Balanced Scorecards) has swelled at particular points in time.

3. What are your thoughts on the relationship between Performance Management at organizational, departmental and individual level?

This is one of the great unknowns that deserve much more academic study. How do the financial measures used predominantly at the corporate level get translated to and from the more operational measures that are used to manage at the lower levels of the organization?

4. What are the 2012 key trends in Performance Management from the perspective of your knowledge and experience in this field?

There has been a lot of progress in understanding which nonfinancial measures of performance are leading indicators of financial (and stock market) performance. There is also a broader conceptualization of Performance Management, to include specific goals, such as environmental (social responsibility) performance.

5. What aspects of Performance Management should be explored more through research?

There are lots of possibilities here. The topic I would put on the top of the list is how to build a combination-of-measures system. Financial measures, by themselves, are insufficient. With what measures should they be supplemented in various settings, and how should all the various measures included be weighted in importance?

6. Please provide some examples of organizations which you would recommend for study due to their approach to Performance Management and achievements.

It is difficult to say which organizations are doing the best job in this area. I would suggest studying organizations that are generally recognized to be well-run, such as the "most admired" list that is published in the U.S. I would also suggest studying organizations that are doing something different—the outliers—as they might be developing the innovative practice that will lead us to something better.

7. Which are the main challenges of Performance Management in practice today?

It is a complex area. There are lots of dimensions of Performance Management. Clearly organizations of different types should not be doing everything the same way. There are even multiple good alternatives for organizations of the same type ("equifinality"). And it is difficult to measure success. So practice in this area is guided by judgment and intuition, rather than by hard scientific findings. Perhaps some of what is being done is merely folklore, not fact. It is hard to sort it all out.

8. What do you think should be improved in the use of Performance Management tools and processes?

I think there is a rush to pushes of new products being sold by consulting firms (e.g., balanced scorecards, beyond budgeting) without a firm understanding of the phenomena underlying them. We need a lot more scientific research.

9. What would you consider best practice in Performance Management?

What the best-run companies are doing. It's a mix of financial and nonfinancial measures and short-run and long-run incentives, with clear goals and useful feedback. It is hard to say more than that.

10. Which aspects of Performance Management should be emphasized during educational programs?

Many educational programs emphasize memorization of terms and practice on very simple problems. Instead, I think we should be trying, first and foremost, to help students cope with what they will face in the complex real world. Throw real, complex problems at them. Help them develop their abilities to sort through the complexity—their problem finding, critical thinking and problem solving skills. There are trade-offs to almost every approach. Students should practice understanding those trade-offs.

11. What are the barriers to achieving higher levels of proficiency in Performance Management among practitioners?

I think the most important one,

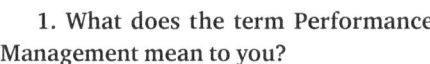

There are lots of dimensions of Performance Management. There are even multiple good alternatives for organizations of the same type ("equifinality"). And it is difficult to measure success. So practice is guided by judgment and intuition, rather than by hard scientific findings.

probably, is that financial measurement is dictated by the rules defined for financial reporting purposes. Those rules are not optimally designed for use in managing an organization, yet most organizations seem bound by them. Also, there is a disconnection between the financial approach to Performance Management (run by accountants) and the operational approach (run by engineers, marketing people, etc.). If we had integrated programs teaching "Performance Management", we could integrate these approaches.

12. What Performance Management question would you like to have answered?

In any given setting, how should we combine financial, market and nonfinancial measures into an optimal Performance Management System?

13. We are developing a database of Performance Management subjects and

degrees in Performance Management. What are your suggestions relevant to the database (i.e. subjects or degreed such as the Masters in Managing Organizational Performance)?

I would look at the work of the Performance Management Association (www.performanceportal.org) and the people in that organization. Their focus is the closest to what you have in mind, and they are doing some good work. ▧

Interviewee name:
Enrique Romero Zabaleta
Title:
Operations Director Mexico & LATAM
Organization:
Insightforce Strategy Management Consultants
Country:
Mexico
Continent:
Nouth America

strategies, well communicated to different areas, with well-defined projects and responsibility in order to focus efforts and achieve the expected results are key.

If you're working in developing countries, I would say that it will be more focused on inventory, production and distribution operations with key performance indicators. It depends on which country you are working in, type of business and social maturity.

1. What does the term Performance Management mean to you?

To me, it means the correct management of resources in order to obtain the expected results on a particular project, business, government issues, etc.

2. What drives interest in Performance Management?

As leaders, we need to make things right, obviously. We need to contribute to society and cover our personal performance ambition. To achieve that, Performance Management skills are a must, to any leader that wants to achieve results.

3. What are your thoughts on the relationship between Performance Management at organizational, departmental and individual level?

Well, at organizational level, I would say that leadership or leaders need to all lined up resources to achieve its expected results in a specific business or project.

At area level, I would say that the people who are involved or committed to a project

need to work all together to go to the overall result of the company or the project, so they have to be working together to achieve the expected results.

As an individual, you have to be an important part in the good performance of the processes to achieve group objectives. I would say it in one word: commitment.

> As leaders, we need to make things right obviously. So we need to contribute to society and cover our personal performance ambition. To achieve that, Performance Management skills are a must to any leader that wants to achieve results.

Really passion for what you do.

4. What are the 2012 key trends in Performance Management from the perspective of your knowledge and experience in this field?

It depends on the country that you are working in. In developed countries I would say strategy is crucial, how to develop clear

5. What aspects of Performance Management should be explored more through research?

From my experience working with management boards, I would say the direct relationship between leadership, right objectives and labor force.

It is really important to work together between leaders and labor force. As I mentioned before, it depends on where you are working. In Europe, this relationship is more advanced than in Latin America. In Latin America, leaders have to work more with the labor force, clarify their vision (strategy) and the communication process.

6. Please provide some examples of organizations which you would recommend for study due to their approach to Performance Management and achievements.

There are plenty of examples. I would say BIMBO is an incredible example of Performance Management Execution and the relationship with their labor force. It's the biggest bakery company in the world. It's Mexican. It's very advanced in how they work with the Performance Management and how they work with the labor force. Every person who works in BIMBO in Mexico, Latin America is very proud of working for that company. This is the key point that differentiates BIMBO from other companies.

There are some companies like BIMBO in developing markets, but it's as usual as it is in developed markets.

Another example would be TETRAPAK, a Swedish company.

TETRAPAK is a leading developer, manufacturer and marketer of packaging material, complete systems for processing, packaging and distribution for liquid food products, It's a good example of efficiency and focus strategy.

7. Which are the main challenges of Performance Management in practice today?

I would say that the world has changed. Now the operations of the companies are globally. Due to global markets and operations worldwide, we are experimenting an increase in the challenges to standardize and focus on a global strategy, find the talent and implement the overall KPIs in each country.

Twenty years ago, companies worked locally, their staff worked locally, mainly suppliers where located in the same country with the same culture and idiosyncrasy.

Today we are part of a global open market, with global customers, with global operations.

The main challenges of Performance Management would be to work with these issues at the same time in different markets and countries.

8. What do you think should be improved in the use of Performance Management tools and processes?

From my experience in Europe and Latin America, I would say again that it's really different, if you work in a developed market or in a developing market.

In first world countries, where business processes and culture are more stabilized, you have to be more focused on strategy and R&D investments.

In developing countries, business process management or Key Performance Indicators and IT investment are the main challenges for the near future.

9. What would you consider best practice in Performance Management?

Performance best practice = vision and strategy communication.

There are plenty of good examples where companies have a good strategy with solid business plans but, the communication of

> Today we are part of a global open market, with global customers, with global operations. The main challenges of Performance Management would be to work with these issues at the same time, in different markets and countries.

it to the different levels of the organization leaves many questions.

Thus, the communication and implementation of the strategy would be also very important. Please take into account in the phase of strategy implementation the differentiation between human resources from different parts of the world, cculture etc.

10. Which aspects of Performance Management should be emphasized during educational programs?

Leadership, Strategy, Project Management, KPIs, human resources management, results orientation, R&D investments. Obviously, depending on the country, sector, and cultural behavior we need to prioritize the efforts.

> In first world countries, where business processes and culture are more stabilized, you have to be more focused on strategy and R&D investments. In developing countries, business process management or Key Performance Indicators and IT investment are the main challenges for the near future.

I think that undergraduate and MBA teachers have to be connected with the business world, to know exactly what is going on.

Management leaders at all levels of the organization have to be more prepared in

these skills than twenty years ago.

11. What are the barriers to achieving higher levels of proficiency in Performance Management among practitioners?

In Europe, you have a high level of educated population with different profiles, which facilitates the development of business. There is no hunger, so leaders must work more on motivation and innovation issues to achieve results.

In developing countries where lack of talent is more common, leaders must work more on operation efficiency, KPI, BPM projects, training courses, etc.

For both markets, ethical management issues, business image and social contribution are key for the medium and long-term.

12. What Performance Management question would you like to have answered?

As a consultant, I highly recommend to have time to read about new findings of how to manage resources in a better way and using new technologies to be actualized in these issues. But finally, it relies more on good and committed leadership.

So I would like to receive updates and new findings to do things in a better and efficient way.

13. As a consultant, what are the most common issues that your customers raised related to Performance Management?

In Europe or developed countries: strategy issues of performance results affecting the global P&L statements and R&D investments. Clear strategies of where we would like to be in the next five to ten years.

In Latin America, we work more on projects related to BPM, increase on productivity, new organizational charts, SCM, marketing plans, distribution costs, etc. Finally, due to a higher competition, we help our customers in the search for proficiency talent needed to be more competitive. ▪

Interviewee name:
Isela Hernandez
Title:
Strategy Management Officer
Organization:
Cinepolis Corporativo
Country:
Mexico
Continent:
North America

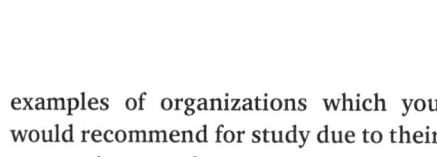

1. What does the term Performance Management mean to you?

Purpose, because it helps to provide a reason to go the extra mile.

2. What drives interest in Performance Management?

Performance Management translates effort into results.

3. What are your thoughts on the relationship between Performance Management at organizational, departmental and individual level?

All have to be aligned to accomplish the organization's success.

4. What are the 2012 key trends in Performance Management from the perspective of your knowledge and experience in this field?

There are three trends:
1. Linkage of personal performance with organizational success and vice versa.
2. Automation.
3. Strategic alignment.

5. What aspects of Performance Management should be explored more through research?

I would say two aspects:
1. Accountability among areas. There are efforts that must be shared.
2. Performance metrics definition; there is literature on how to define good metrics, but it is mostly designed by instinct.

6. Please provide some examples of organizations which you would recommend for study due to their approach to Performance Management and achievements.

Cinepolis, the company I currently work

> Performance Management translates effort to results.

for.

7. Which are the main challenges of Performance Management in practice today?

> In achieving higher levels of proficiency in Performance Management, there are two main barriers: simplicity and alignment, and a clear definition of positions and job duties. Performance Management should be more aware of initiatives and results aligned to strategy, rather than to operational results.

There are two challenges:
1. Alignment across areas/understanding/communication.
2. Feedback and cooperation.

8. What do you think should be improved in the use of Performance Management tools and processes?

Two aspects:
1. Opportunity and flexibility.
2. Automation and analysis (BI, DATA WAREHOUSE).

9. What would you consider best practice in Performance Management?

It's about definition:
1. Definition on time, communication and automation.
2. Clear process definition.

10. Which aspects of Performance Management should be emphasized during educational programs?

Metrics and analysis.

11. What are the barriers to achieving higher levels of proficiency in Performance Management among practitioners?

There are two main barriers:
1. Simplicity and alignment.
2. A clear definition of positions and job duties. Performance Management should be more aware of initiatives and results aligned to strategy, rather than to operational results.

12. What Performance Management question would you like to have answered?

Where does it belong? Strategic Planning or HR?

13 Which were the recent achievements in generating value from Performance Management in your organization?

The recent achievements include:
1. Increased EBITDA.
2. Empowerment.
3. Accountability.
4. Alignment. ▪

Interviewee name:
Humberto E Della Torre
Title:
Information Systems Manager
Organization:
Grupo Calleja
Country:
El Salvador
Continent:
North America

1. What does the term Performance Management mean to you?

Performance Management is a term that describes the internal culture of having an existing permanent practice of monitoring and adjusting business goals for the different organizational entities to drive a continuous improvement program in the enterprise.

2. What drives interest in Performance Management?

The fostering of product and service innovation, excellent customer service and operational efficiency is the driver for our continuous improvement program.

3. What are your thoughts on the relationship between Performance Management at organizational, departmental and individual level?

There are domains of measurements for the different echelons of management with higher or lower levels of variety and/or summarization. While some measurements exist in different domains, with more or less restricted data sub domains according to the intended audience, others are for specific domains that need specialized information for control reasons. Finding the right mix of measurements for each domain and the organizational responsibility distribution is the most challenging part of a Performance Management concept.

4. What are the 2012 key trends in Performance Management from the perspective of your knowledge and experience in this field?

Transform the common business end user insight into business intelligence use cases, to drive corrective or innovation related actions in the business as fast as possible.

5. What aspects of Performance Management should be explored more through research?

I remember reading a whitepaper by MIT Sloan Management Review and the IBM Institute for Business Value that tried to explain how to reach organizational maturity in the business intelligence area recommending focusing on the following skills in the listed order:

- Optimize data visualization.
- Simulations and scenario development.
- Analytics applied within business processes.
- Regression analysis, discrete choice modeling and mathematical optimization.
- Clustering and segmentation.
- Historic trend analysis and forecasting.
- Optimize report organization.

6. Please provide some examples of organizations which you would recommend for study due to their approach to Performance Management and achievements.

I would recommend Siemens A.G. as a good case for study. I was a regional CEO in that organization in the past and had the opportunity to have access and training to a very holistic methodology to implement good corporate governance

The fostering of product and service innovation, excellent customer service and operational efficiency is the driver for our continuous improvement program.

that used Performance Management as the compass to reach the business goals. The methodology was implemented with state-of-the-art application and tools in all related fields of activity related to Performance Management. Unfortunately, I did not have the opportunity to complete the project due to a worldwide organizational crisis that split the organization in two halves during 2007.

7. Which are the main challenges of Performance Management in practice today?

The main challenge is having all the required ingredients available for a good program under one roof.

- Technical Knowledge
- Organizational Knowledge
- Work Methodologies
- Application and Tools
- Data
- Consistent levels of management bandwidth to keep project priority high
- Persistence

8. What do you think should be improved in the use of Performance Management tools and processes?

Within the same whitepaper referenced before the following recommendations were offered for any Performance Management program:

- Prioritization schemas: focus on the biggest and highest value propositions.
- Standardized business functional models: within each opportunity start with questions not data.
- Complex event management: embed insights to drive actions and deliver value.
- Technology integration and upgradability: keep existing capabilities while adding new ones.
- Strategy: use an information agenda for the future.

9. What would you consider best practice in Performance Management?

Measure organizational maturity in process management in a systematic way to validate if Performance Management is being used as a means to create an impact in the way daily business is being done.

10. Which aspects of Performance Management should be emphasized during educational programs?

I believe the following topics should be covered to create a good program for Performance Management professionals:

- Project Management
- Process Management
- Operations Research
- Quality Management
- Data Management
- Implementation Management
- Standardized business process frameworks
  - Concord (CRM)
  - SCOR (SCM)
  - ITIL (P&I)
  - Product Lifecycle Management (PLM)
  - Human Resources Management (HRM)
  - Finance
  - Strategy planning
  - Etc.
- Basic Finance
- Balance Scorecard
- Business Case Analysis

11. What are the barriers to achieving higher levels of proficiency in Performance Management among practitioners?

For me, the biggest barrier in implementing a good Performance Management program is the lack of understanding from management that having a good organizational governance

> For me, the biggest barrier found to implement a good Performance Management program is the lack of understanding from management that having a good organizational governance system is a pre-requisite to start the Performance Management program.

system is a pre-requisite to start the Performance Management program.

12. What Performance Management question would you like to have answered?

I would like to have a worldwide standardized business process framework library for all areas of activity, subject of Performance Management. So far, I do not know about the existence of a PLM (Product Lifecycle management) or HRM (Human Resources Management) process standard framework, for instance.

13. Which were the recent achievements in generating value from Performance Management in your organization?

We are in the process of creating our Balance Scorecard to follow up the performance of the most critical business factors in the organization. Based on the data for the first months of the year, we are going to regulate current goals for more realistic values and create a business strategy later. The initial Balance Scorecard will be in flux until we become satisfied with the defined domains and organizational distribution of responsibility and frequency of reporting.

Still, we are already reaping the benefits of having a very well developed system of business intelligence that helps us to do things like the following:

- Determine the profit margin by the day in spite of having a very complex system of discounts and promotions for products, vendors, customers and distributor.
- Determine the products that are being stolen from our branches the most.
- Measure the customer value for each branch.
- Analyze the market by several hierarchies of interest for the managers.

Interviewee name:
Ricardo Rodriguez-Ulloa
Title:
Principal Lecturer and Researcher
Main subjects:
Systemic Strategic Management
Soft Systems Methodology – SSM
Soft System Dynamics Methodology –
SSDM Management Cybernetics
System Dynamics and Foresight
Studies
Organization:
Centrum Católica, Pontificia
Universidad Católica del Perú
Country:
Peru
Continent:
South America

1. What does the term Performance Management mean to you?

Performance Management for me has to do with how to monitor, control and manage the strategic and operational direction of an organization of any kind.

2. What drives interest in Performance Management?

Nowadays, we are in a very complex social, cultural, political and economic world, besides the climate conditions. So it is very important to monitor the behavior of an organization at strategic and operational level, with diverse kind of indicators which allows to measure its performance along time and space.

3. What are your thoughts on the relationship between Performance Management at organizational, departmental and individual level?

Well, let me tell that when I refer to "diverse kind of indicators", I am referring to efficacy, efficiency, effectiveness, ethics and aesthetics kind of indicators (5 Es), so there should be a very strong relationship among these kinds of indicators with the overall organization (strategic level, tactic level and operational level). This as well must be aligned with the performance of individuals within organizations, because the organization's interests and the individuals' interests must go hand in hand in order to get best results.

4. What are the 2012 key trends in Performance Management from the perspective of your knowledge and experience in this field?

Your question is very interesting, because it allows me to mention the kind of indicators to measure the performance of organizations and manage them is changing since some years ago. From hard kind of indicators (those which measure finance, productivity, production, market share and so on) to more softer indicators which can measure the culture level of development of an oorganization. This helps to see if, for example, an organization is prepared for a strategic change or how the power is distributed within the organization or what about the mental models of the people who have the power to decide strategic issues in the organization. This is only thinking about the inside of the organization. There should be also other types of soft indicators to measure and see their trends, concerning the environment, as the political climate, the cultural factors in favor or not of the

implementation of a business idea and so on.

Besides that, what we really need is the combination of both categories of indicators, using them in the synergistic way.

I think that in the next years, this kind of indicators will be used or need to be used in most organizations around the world. I am not mentioning, for example, the issue of corporate social responsibility, but only thinking about this issue, there are a lot of soft kind indicators to be considered. The complex problems we are facing around the world, like problems with the environment, are forcing us to start thinking that we need to measure other kind of variables, which were not considered in the past.

5. What aspects of Performance Management should be explored more through research?

Precisely, those soft kind of indicators. There is a need to do more research on this issue to define the right kind of indicators. An additional aspect is to develop technology to be used in measuring those indicators

There, I think that other kind of technology is needed as well. For example, the use of systemic methodologies and technologies, as system dynamics or the use of artificial intelligence would be needed to measure the conjunction effect of a myriad of indicators, in order to measure the organization´s performance.

6. Please provide some examples of organizations which you would recommend for study due to their approach to Performance Management and achievements.

Well, in my environment here in Peru, there are several organizations which would be interesting to study. An example is Ajegroup, a Peruvian group which started in the Peruvian highlands as a small family business and now is on Asian, American and European markets.

Another one would be our Business School, Centrum Catolica Business School. In less than 10 years, we obtained the three corns, which is not an easy task for many business schools around the world.

Let me mention a Peruvian bank, Interbank, which is now operating around the world, but mainly in China. They are

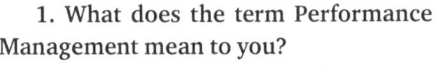
Performance Management for me has to do with how to monitor, control and manage the strategic and operational direction of an organization of any kind.

growing with a very smart strategy. And I suppose they are measuring their indicators very carefully.

7. Which are the main challenges of Performance Management in practice today?

The main problem is complexity. We are in the complexity era. Everything is complex. To educate a child who is born today is complex. How to educate him or her so that they are viable in the next 50 or 80 years? What kind of things should we teach them?

Now, managing an organization of any kind and size is a complex issue. We do not have market barriers with the Internet. Most business is done and will be done by Internet. The virtual organization exists now. And everything will be in the virtual world, where the distance is a click, like now we are in this interview. So there are a lot of challenges in developing the Performance Management discipline, a lot of field of research on the topic.

8. What do you think should be improved in the use of Performance Management tools and processes?

You need to work on several things: develop philosophy, develop concepts, develop theory, develop mythologies and develop technology, in order to have the adequate tools for performance monitoring and process modeling of any kind of organizations. This also applies to networks of organizations, because an important issue in this century is the concept of network, because network brings you synergy. The great factor we need to measure is synergy of organizations and networks.

9. What would you consider best practice in Performance Management?

Well I should mention:

1. A consensual understand among stakeholders of a situation about what we mean with a specific indicator (hard or soft indicator).

2. Constancy and discipline in order to obtain the trend of the behavior of the defined indicators use in a specific case.

3. The use of tools and technology in order to automate, as far as possible, the framework used to permanently measure the organization's performance. These tools must look the trends of the indicators in the past, the present and the future of the organizations and its environment.

4. An open minded work team able to work in group.

5. Applying the concept of learning in an organization is a never-ending process.

> When I refer to "diverse kind of indicators", I am referring to efficacy, efficiency, effectiveness, ethics and aesthetics kind of indicators (5 Es), so there should be a very strong relationship among these kinds of indicators with the overall organization (strategic level, tactic level and operational level).

10. Which aspects of Performance Management should be emphasized during educational programs?

I think that there are some neglected areas in educational programs, which need to be considered in the XXI-st century:

1. Critical Thinking. The practice of thinking in a critical way. This is a very urgent need due to the positive and objective paradigm installed in our society.

2. A shift of the positive and reductionist approach in study organizations, to a more phenomenological and hermeneutic approach.

> We are in the complexity era. Everything is complex. To educate a child who is born today is complex. How to educate him or her so that they are viable in the next 50 or 80 years? What kind of things should we teach them?

3. The practice of systemic approaches in studying organizations.

4. The use of imagination and creativity.

5. In consequence, Innovation.

6. Future studies.

11. What are the barriers to achieving higher levels of proficiency in Performance Management among practitioners?

I think there are at least three barriers:

1. The lack of critical thinking (everyone thinks that they are right! A consequence of the positive paradigm which dominates nowadays).

2. The lack of integral methodologies to guide the overall process of implementing Performance Management approaches in organizations.

3. The lack of a smart technology to manage the complexity of measurement and analyze trends of a myriad of indicators in organizations and their environment. The role of artificial intelligence is a key factor in this.

12. What Performance Management question would you like to have answered?

I think that I have not only one, but three that I am concerned with:

1.What indicators should be used, in order to have an overall view of the organization, from a phenomenological and hermeneutic view?

2. Which should be the methodology to measure them?

3. What should be the technology(ies) I would need to use, in order to obtain this overall (systemic) view of the organization and its environment?

13. We are developing a database of Performance Management subjects and degrees in Performance Management. What are your suggestions relevant to the database (i.e. subjects or degrees such as the Masters in Managing Organizational Performance)?

I think this is very important. However, there should be some kind of alignment in the database between the paradigm, the philosophical framework of studying organizations and the concrete indicators. On the other hand, as I mentioned before, there should be an alignment between the organization's indicators and the individual indicators that are to be measured. ▪

Map Overview

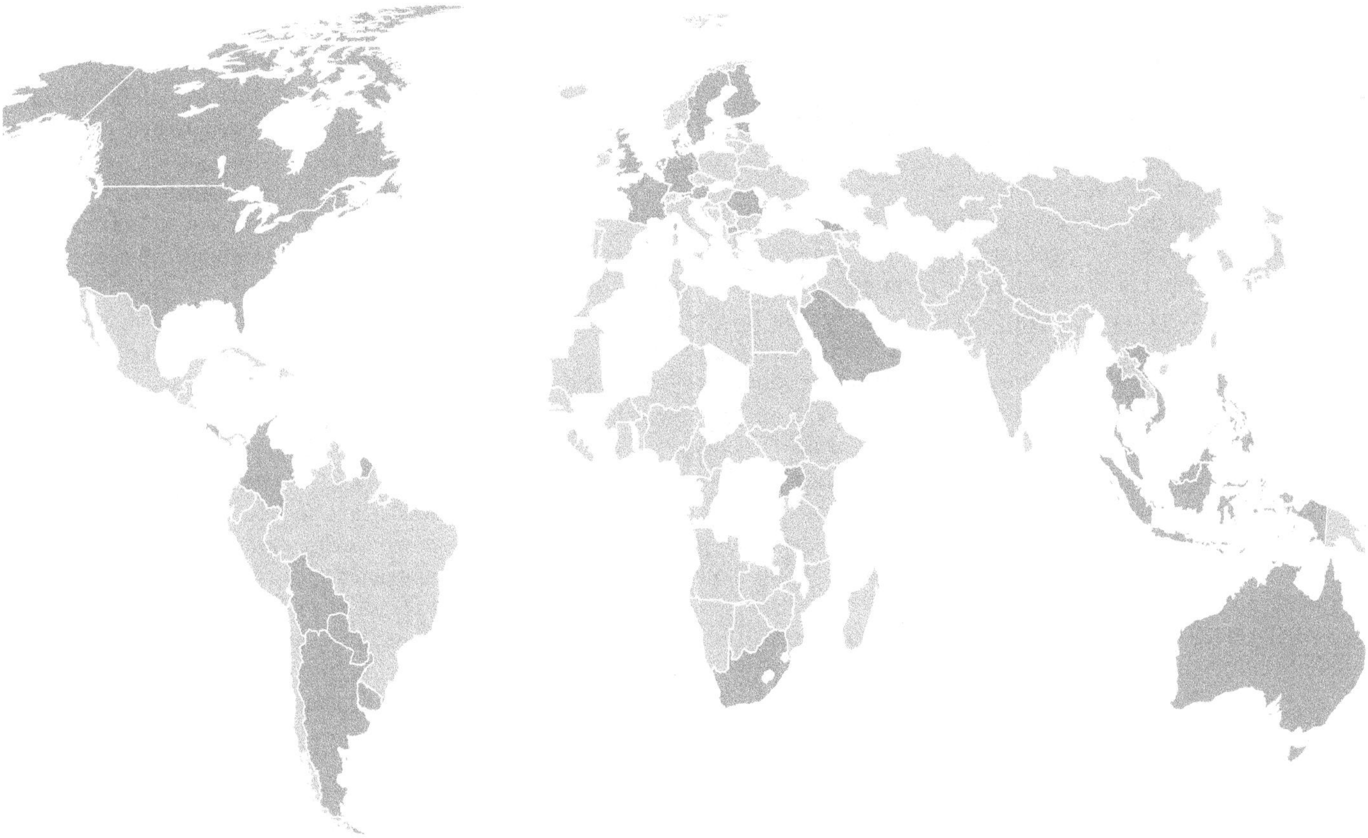

Legislated   Plan

Introduction

Performance Management as a discipline, practice and area of study is growing in popularity every year. Public and private organizations in countries all over the world are gradually embracing the concepts of balance and alignment as they seek new ways to improve their internal processes, thus the quality of the output. The KPI Institute has researched the status of performance management in over 150 countries, exploring legislation or other Performance Management policies that have been implemented to guide organizations at national level towards adopting performance management practices.

While it is not surprising to see the governments of major countries with large populations and high GDPs implementing different Performance Management strategies, it is interesting to see which smaller or developing countries have also implemented Performance Management systems.

The map above illustrates the type of performance management practices adoption for each of the countries reviewed: legislation and plans to implement performance management systems, policies, acts, projects, systems, essentially anything affiliated with Performance Management implementation at the public level. A full list of all the countries that were covered in the research follows.

It provides an overview of the type of Performance Management practices and legislations that different countries from different continents have either introduced or are in the process of implementing.

Country Profiles

Some of the most representative countries in terms of performance management legislation and national emphasis are:

Australia
- The Management Advisory Committee considers a number of management issues where analysis, discussion and the identification of better practical approaches would inform and promote improvements in public administration.
- Changes to the budgetary process to provide additional managerial autonomy within a firm has also been a key aspect of Performance Management.
- Considerable emphasis is being placed on benchmarking performance.
- Contestability is receiving substantially increased attention as a means of improving the economy, effectiveness and responsiveness of services.

Canada
- Canada's Performance 2010–2011 is an annual report tabled in Parliament by the President of the Treasury Board.
- Based on the key findings and recommendations from consultations held in 2010, this year's edition provides a snapshot of the government's contribution to the prosperity and well-being of Canadians, with an emphasis on four broad key issues: demographic change, northern potential, economic prosperity and domestic security.

China
- Since the mid-1980s, the Chinese government has implemented a Performance Management regime that has grown in complexity and sophistication.
- Emerging first at the local government level, China's Objective Responsibility System (ORS) involves setting objectives for subordinate government units and holding individual leaders responsible for their achievement.

Kenya
- In April 2008, the Coalition Government formed the Public Sector Reforms and Performance Contracting (PSR&PC).

- The programme is currently supported by the Government of Kenya, the World Bank, the United Nations Development Programme and the Governments of Canada, Denmark, Finland, Sweden, and the UK.

Mozambique
- Performance Management Systems in the Mozambican Public Service have been funded by the World Bank and the Government of Mozambique.
- The Country Program Evaluation (CPE) assessed the overall performance and results of a five-year project based on the Canadian International Development Agency's (CIDA) latest Country Development Programming Framework (CDPF) for Mozambique.

Romania
- In Romania, Law no. 40/2011 for amending and supplementing the Labour code established the right and duty of employers for setting performance criteria for employees.
- The employer has now the right to establish individual performance objectives, as well as the criteria for evaluating their achievement.

Malaysia
- The Performance Management & Delivery Unit (PEMANDU) was established in 2009 as a unit under the Prime Minister's Department. Its main role is to oversee implementation and assess progress of the Economic Transformation Programme and the Government Transformation Programme. It facilitates and supports the delivery of the national key result area (NKEAs), national key economic areas (NKRAs) and ministerial key result area (MKRAs).

United Kingdom
- The British Performance Management model has largely been centralized, top-down, with lower tier organizations mandated, either legally or administratively, to produce performance reporting data.
- The Public Service Agreements System (PSAs) have come to be seen as an international model for setting performance targets, broadly linked to the budgeting process.

United States of America
- The US government deployed Performance Management systems as mandated by the Government Performance and Results Act of 1993 (GPRA). ▣

Country Legislation

Country	Category	Notes
Afghanistan	Plan	The Performance Manage Plan (PMP) is the U.S. Mission in Afghanistan's tool to plan and manage the process of assessing and reporting progress towards assistance/foreign policy objectives identified by the President of the United States, the Secretary of State, the U.S. Ambassador to Afghanistan, and the Government of Islamic Republic of Afghanistan. *Source: http://afghanistan.usaid.gov/en/about/performance_monitoring*
Albania	Plan	A separate project on Performance Management for local government was developed with UNOPS Albania (Art Gold 2 Albania). It should be discussed and agreed with UNOPS management centre at FAO in Rome for possible implementation in Albania in 2011. *Source: http://www.un.org.al/*
American Samoa	Legislated	Has established a government Performance Results Act of 1993. *Source: http://www.whitehouse.gov/omb/mgmt-gpra/gplaw2m*
Angola	Plan	There have been recommendations by various global organizations (eg. UNDP and USAID) for the development of Performance Management practices in the country to better facilitate efficient foreign aid and working practices. *Source: http://www.usaid.gov/oig/public/fy12rpts/4-654-12-006-p.pdf*
Anguilla	Plan	The Department of Public Administration is committed to the implementation of a Performance Management System (PMS) at the beginning of 2012. It is a system that has been designed to improve overall performance and productivity of the public service by actively linking individual work performance to department/ministry, organizational and national goals. *Source: http://www.anguillanews.com/enews/index.php/permalink/4139.html*
Antarctica	Legislated	The Australian Government has a Expeditioner Performance Appraisal Scheme (EPAS) which uses the Antarctic Service Code of Personal Behaviour as the basis for assessment of performance. The EPAS is designed to facilitate objective assessment of the technical skills and behaviours exhibited by the expeditioner from the commencement of employment until their return to Australia. While the Antarctic arm of the Australia government also has a Human Resources section which deals with Performance Management schemes. *Sources: http://www.antarctica.gov.au/__data/assets/pdf_file/0005/38876/Expeditioner-Handbook-April-2011-FINAL.pdf and http://www.antarctica.gov.au/__data/assets/pdf_file/0009/39186/APPENDIX-5-AAD-BRANCHES-AND-SECTIONS.pdf*
Antigua and Barbuda	Plan	The education department in Antigua and Barbuda had "previously implemented the Excel-based Performance Management Tool (PMT) developed by OERU, also on a pilot basis. Although the PMT was not adopted on a systemwide basis, several schools involved in the pilot test continue to use the PMT templates to record and present data". They are now using the AbusSTAR system developed in Barbados. *Source: http://ddp-ext.worldbank.org/EdStats/ATGpro09.pdf*
Argentina	Legislated	Argentina's PFMS was created in 1992 with the objectives of informing the budget allocation process, encouraging agencies' management improvement, and enhancing transparency and accountability... On the other hand, the creation of SIEMPRO in 1995, also in Argentina, was part of a broader initiative intended to enhance the government's capacity to develop and implement effective policies - in this particular case, in the domain of anti-poverty policies... Also Results-Based Management System's Monitoring Scheme... All three systems were enacted under laws and decrees by the government. *Source: http://siteresources.worldbank.org/INTEVACAPDEV/Resources/4585664-1254408803979/experience_inst_lac.pdf*
Armenia	Legislated	The Armenia LGP (Local Government Program) II was competitively awarded to UI as an extension to the three-year, $4 million LGP I, also carried out by UI. This second phase of the local government capacity building and reform effort in Armenia continues the basic orientation of the phase one program. This includes local government management and service improvement, citizen participation and legal framework and decentralization. LGP II incorporates an additional focus on economic development strategies, citizen participation with greater emphasis on gender and youth involvement, asset management, apartment building management, and Performance Management. *Source: http://www.urban.org/center/idg/projects/pdescrip.cfm?ProjectID=301*

Country	Category	Notes
Aruba	Plan	The European Development Fund report states that there are preparations for the installation of an Education Management Information System towards the end of 2011... and the introduction of a national student tracking management system... performance monitoring was identified as an area to be strengthened. *Source: http://ec.europa.eu/europeaid/where/octs_and_greenland/documents/spd_final_aruba_en.pdf*
Australia	Legislated	For several decades, performance measurement has been used as an internal informational tool to evaluate departmental operations nd make program and budgetary decisions (Ho and Ni, 2005). In the public sector, interest in performance neasures has grown enormously, as evidenced by the large literature on new public management (NPM), benchmarking and balanced scorecards. The Australian government pursued the commencement of a public sector reform in 1993, which considered the need to achieve a performance culture within the sector. " *Source: http://www.cpaaustralia.com.au/cps/rde/xbcr/cpa-site/measuring-public-sector-performance-study.pdf* The Management Advisory Committee (MAC) is a forum of Secretaries and Agency Heads established under the Public Service Act 1999 to advise the Australian Government on matters relating to the management of the Australian Public Service (APS). In addressing its broad advisory function the Committee considers a number of management issues where analysis, discussion, and the identification of better practice approaches would inform and promote improvements in public administration. *Source: http://www.apsc.gov.au/mac/index.html*
Austria	Legislated	Primarily related to their budget expemnditure process, where Performance Management is used by the ministries, Federal Chancellery and Parliament in order to generate the Medium-Term Expenditure Framework (MTEF)... Performance Management is far more than performance budgeting. The Performance Management cycle is about planning, implementing and evaluating outcomes and outputs. Based on the programme of the federal government politicians define strategic objectives and outcomes. Public administration then has to determine the necessary outputs in order to achieve the desired outcomes. *Source: http://www.bka.gv.at/DocView.axd?CobId=42860*
Azerbaijan	Plan	UNDP is committed to results and risk-based Performance Management, as well as the values and culture of accountability and transparency. UNDP Azerbaijan manages its programme and operations in line with the applicable UNDP accountability framework and oversight policy. *Source: http://www.un-az.org/undp/sehife.php?lang=eng&page=0100*
Bahrain	Plan	The Kingdom of Bahrain is very supportive of the implementation of Performance Management systems as evidenced by their visiting of UAE in 2012 in order to inspect their successful Performance Management systems and as outlined by McKinsey's report on their new vision for an implementation of a PM system in 2008. *Source: http://www.fahr.gov.ae/Portal/en/news/1/3/2012/bahraini-delegation-hosted-by-fahr.aspx*
Bangladesh	Plan	The Ministry of Establishment, Government of Bangladesh, is carrying out the MATT 2 (Managing At The Top 2) program in close collaboration with DFID. It is envisaged that the joint efforts will develop reformed human resource management systems within the Bangladesh Civil Service as an important structure to drive administrative reform. MATT 2 aims to create a critical mass of reform-minded civil service top managers to help bringing fundamental improvements in the governance of Bangladesh. *Source: http://extension.ait.ac.th/course/299*
Barbados	Plan	Public Sector Reform (PSR) Initiatives PSR is vital if Barbados wants to compete in the regional, hemispheric and global environment. To this end, a number of significant reform initiatives to strengthen the public service and make it more professional were introduced: * Performance Management * Performance Review and Development System (PRDS) * Job Evaluation Exercise * Human Resources Management Information System (SmartStream) * Employee Assistance Programme (EAP) * Humanised Management/Personnel Excellence Programme * Service Assessment and Improvement Programme *Source: http://www.reform.gov.bb/page/Public%20Sector%20Reform%20in%20Barbados.pdf*

Country	Category	Notes
Belarus	Plan	A recent report published the UN states that there will be performance evaluation in order to to improve the performance of state employees, selection and collocation of the civil service cadre qualification exams will take place. An employee is obliged to take the first exam after three years. Consequently the exam is taken every three years and is managed by a commission assigned for the purpose. *Source: http://unpan1.un.org/intradoc/groups/public/documents/un/unpan023207.pdf*
Belgium	Plan	Performance contracts are embedded in an overall Performance Management strategy of the Flemish government. But in many cases, the contract is just another way of controlling already excsting para-departmental organizations as the case of the Flemish Service for Job Mediation and Vocational Training shows. The legal status of performance contracts remains an unresolved issue at both levels of gavovernment. *Source: http://www.oecd.org/dataoecd/11/53/1902940.pdf*
Belize	Plan	1997 saw the initiation and adoption of a new Performance Appraisal System for the Belize Public Service. The system is designed to complement administrative and personnel factors such as strategic plans, performance agreements and continuous feedback and interaction between supervisor and co-workers. *Source: http://unpan1.un.org/intradoc/groups/public/documents/caricad/unpan000475.pdf*
Benin	Legislated	Benin adopted the Performance-Based Management (PBM) reform in 1999. The primary objective of the reform is to initiate a process of gradual transition from resource-based budget management to budget management focused on objectives.This transition will be achieve through (i) increased accountability of spending in ministries in the preparation, execution, and monitoring and evaluation of their Program Budgets (PBs) in the context of performance-based management, and (ii) the strategic, efficient, and equitable use of all public resources with a view to promoting growth and improving the living conditions of the people, and thereby reducing proverty in Benin. *Source: http://www.mfdr.org/sourcebook/2ndEdition/4-5BeninRBM.pdf*
Bermuda	Plan	Bermuda Police Service would implement a computerised performance and development appraisal system that would provide a comprehensive and continuous evidence-based performance review for every officer up to the rank of superintendent. *Source: http://www.royalgazette.com/article/20110323/NEWS/703239943/-1/news&source=RSS*
Bhutan	Plan	The performance appraisal system covers all government employees, including personnel on probation and contract. *Source: http://www.bhutanobserver.bt/performance-appraisal-still-weak/*
Bolivia	Legislated	Bolivia's Performance Management and budgeting reform agenda has been expansive and ambitious. The effort started in the late 1980s with the introduction of the Integrated Financial Management project in 1987. Three years later, the Law of Financial Management and Control was stipulated with the intention to focus managers on results, transparency, and accountability. The law required all ministries prepare annual operating plans complemented with performance indicators and targets which provided the basis of budgeting decisions and performance evaluation. In the 1990s, education-sector reform (1994) and the health sector reform (1999) carried along the performance orientation in the central government. However, the reform agenda suffered from very limited implementation at the close of 1990s. In 1998/99, the Institutional Reform Project (IRP) was introduced to curb corruption and also to restore the reform momentum in performance orientation. It affected public budgeting and financial management in two areas (1) developing an integrated financial management system (SIMGMA) and (2) boosting a results-oriented strategic budgeting and management processes (Montes and Andrews 2005).
Bosnia and Herzegovina	Plan	Recently implemented an enhancement of efficacy, efficiency, effectiveness and responsibility in work on the civil service bodies through improvement of the existing Performance Management system at different levels of government in BiH... this was to ensure support for the Action Plan 1 for implementation of the public administration reform in BiH where by contributing to implementation of the Public Reform Administration Strategy with the objective of fulfilling the requirements for membership in the European Union. *Source: http://parco.gov.ba/eng/?page=388*

Country	Category	Notes
Botswana	Plan	1. Performance Management systems are currently in place in Botswana, Ghana, South Africa and Uganda. Source: http://www.uneca.org/publications/dpmd/public_sector_mangt.pdf 2. Supported the policy and planning aspects of a Pay Based Reward System to link the government's Performance Management System implementation strategy with the performance of individual Public Officers. *Source: http://www.fmp.ca/interna.htm*
Brazil	Plan	Brazil has the legal order to establish the individual performance evaluation system under Brazilian Public Administration. *Source: http://www.oecd.org/dataoecd/0/47/39612276.pdf*
Brunei	Plan	Human Resource Management initiatives include the Performance Appraisal System in the Brunei Civil Service that is currently tied to Annual Bonuses awarded every December. Apart from the Performance Appraisal System, the Brunei Civil Service also has provisions for all civil servants in the form of a variety of government benefits such as the Subsistence Allowance added on to basic civil service salaries, passage allowances which consist of three-yearly passage allowances as well as a ten-yearly passage allowance to London and a fifteen-yearly passage allowance to perform the Hal pilgrimage to Mecca. *Source: http://www.bruneiresources.com/pdf/accsm14_brunei_paper.pdf*
Bulgaria	Plan	In 2006 - 2007, the Centre of Expertise worked with the NAMRB to pilot a Performance Management programme in Bulgaria, focusing on local economic development and communications. Six pilot municipalities participated in the project: Ruse, Kurdjali, Strumiani, Dobrich, Gabrovo and Pazardjik. Performance measurement and management tools including a template with a number of performance indicators were prepared and adjusted to each pilot local authority's specific environment (its own priorities, objectives and targets). Internal systems for measuring performance were established in each pilot municipality with support from NAMRB. According to information provided from NAMRB, since June 2006, four of these municipalities have been using their templates to take systematic stock of their performance in local economic development and three pilots in communications. *Source: http://www.namrb.org/doc/namrbProject.doc*
Burkina Faso	Plan	After adopting structural adjustment plans during the 1990s, Burkina Faso began a poverty reduction programme in 2000 by adopting a Poverty Reduction Strategy Paper (PRSP). Since 2000, Burkina Faso has been drawing up a three-year rolling Medium-Term Expenditure Framework (MTEF), with a view to strengthening the implementation of Results-oriented Public Expenditure Management started in 1999 as a new method for preparing and executing the Government Budget. *Source: http://www.kms1.isn.ethz.ch/serviceengine/Files/ISN/96628/wp207.pdf*
Burma	N/A	AUSAID highlights that "insufficient attention has been paid to collecting and assessing performance information and this limits the programs' ability to demonstrate aid effectiveness. Undertaking rigorous evaluation has been difficult because of a lack of reliable national data and socio-economic statistics in Burma... The Burma Program is part of this and is developing clear strategic directions and results-based performance frameworks. *Source: http://www.ausaid.gov.au/Publications/Documents/burma-dcr-2010.pdf*
Burundi	Plan	The US Government alongside USAID will aid the Burundi Government from 2011-2015 in order to develop a global health initiative action plan which includes key benchmarks and timelines (see Monitoring and Evaluation). ... The action plan will be created in accordance with the development of a GHI logical framework and Performance Management Plan (PMP), including the selection of performance indicators, both standard (GOB, USG/FACTS, USG/FtF, etc.) and individual (GOB, USG/FACTS). *Source: http://www.ghi.gov/documents/organization/175128.pdf*
Cambodia	Legislated	In Cambodia, the government and development partners implemented the Merit Based Payment Initiative in 2005 within the Ministry of Economy and Finance, with plans to expand to other ministries including the Ministry of Health. The program rewards civil servants with higher pay in accordance with their merit, and is accompanied by a rigorous Performance Management system. *Source: http://www.biomedcentral.com/1478-4491/6/18*

Country	Category	Notes
Cameroon	Plan	Two management systems created in Cameroon in collaboration with the World Bank: "In close collaboration with the Ministry of Basic Education, the World Bank launched in 2011 an initiative with the objective to prepare education report cards (produced at school, district and regional levels) with comparative data on context (urban/rural, road accessibility, distance to health center…), available resources (teachers, textbooks, school grants…) and performance (exam pass rates, drop-out rates, repetition rates, parity ratios…) availed to different management levels and to schools." and "Piloted in the Adamawa and North West Regions, the Budget Transparency Initiative promotes budget transparency at multiple levels – from schools and health centers to local councils, divisions, and regions. Through simplification, analysis and dissemination of budget information the initiative seeks to raise awareness and build capacity among government officials and local institutions to engage in dialogue with citizens around budgetary issues, and to encourage demand for good governance. *Source: http://web.worldbank.org/WBSITE/EXTERNAL/COUNTRIES/AFRICAEXT/CAMEROONE XTN/0,,contentMDK:23171022~menuPK:50003484~pagePK:2865066~piPK:2865079~theSite PK:343813,00.html*
Canada	Legislated	The Management Accountability Framework (MAF) was introduced in 2004 to improve organizational capability in 10 core management disciplines (e.g. risk management, citizen-focused service) based on 21 sub-elements, or indicators. Released in the fall of 2011, Canada's Performance 2010–11 is an annual report tabled in Parliament by the President of the Treasury Board. Based on the key findings and recommendations from consultations held in 2010, this year's edition provides a snapshot of the government's contribution to the prosperity and well-being of Canadians over the 2010–11 fiscal year, with an emphasis on four broad key issues: demographic change, northern potential, economic prosperity, and domestic security. *Sources: http://www.instituteforgovernment.org.uk/pdfs/casestudy_canada.pdf and http://www. tbs-sct.gc.ca/reports-rapports/cp-rc/index-eng.asp*
Cayman Islands	Plan	Has numerous management performance initiatives: Output & ownership management… Staff Performance Management… Advanced management techniques and systems e.g., Business Process Re-engineering, Productivity Improvement Programmes, Customer Service Improvement Programmes. Cost Benefit Analysis, Activity Based Costing, Project Appraisal, Quality Improvement" and in education Performance Management of Educators in CIG schools, Performance Management in other education systems, performance related pay. *Sources: http://www.cayman.gov.ky/pls/portal30/docs/FOLDER/PERSONNEL/RECRUITMENT/ JOB_DESCRIPTIONS/V08207.DOC and http://www.education.gov.ky/pls/portal/ docs/PAGE/MEHHOME/EDUCATION/FEATURES/EDUCATORSCONDITIONSREPORT/ FINALEDUCATORSREPORT.PDF*
Central African Republic	Plan	USAID has its own Central African Regional Program for the Environment in CAR and has its own CARPE II Performance Management Plan and Results Framework. *Source: http://redlac.org/carpe_pmp.pdf*
Chile	Plan	Has many Pay for Performance initiatives and also compares itself with Mexico. *Sources: http://www.mfdr.org/sourcebook/2ndEdition/4-1ChilePS.pdf and www.moph.go.th/ops/ hrdj/hrdj10/document/chile-James.doc*

Country	Category	Notes
China	Legislated	From at least the mid-1980s the Chinese government has implemented a Performance Management regime that has grown in complexity and sophistication. Emerging first at local government level, China's 'objective responsibility system' (ORS) involved setting objectives for subordinate government units and holding individual leaders responsible for their fulfillment." Source: http://blog-pfm.imf.org/pfmblog/2010/09/performance-management-in-china-a-gradual-evolution.html "Since the mid-1990s, in step with the market economy, China's Performance Management system has developed relatively quickly. Officials have provided incentives to improve performance embedded in the human resource management system. Although there was an initial heavy emphasis on economic growth, this emphasis has given way to targets that focus on social and public service functions, sustainable development, and administration by law – a welcome development. We have seen that initiatives to improve Performance Management have come from both the centre in a top-down style and from local governments. As they sought to better position themselves, local governments have been active in identifying performance-enhancing strategies, sometimes only symbolically. China's experience of the objective responsibility system indicates that further efforts are needed to encourage collaborative arrangements to address pressing public problems, such as environmental protection and water conservation. More effort is also needed to focus on policy outcomes and try to bring outcomes into the Performance Management equation. Finally, enhancing public participation in China's Performance Management regime will strengthen its legitimacy and help to ensure that government programmes are effectively meeting human development needs. *Source: http://www.oecd.org/dataoecd/26/63/48169592.pdf*
Christmas Island	Legislated	The Australian Government has enacted 'performance measures' for the Christmas Island National Park... also has Performance Management systems for the provider of its detention centres Serco "The Contract also specifies that Serco must meet or exceed the Indicator Metrics and Key Performance Indicators expressed in the Contract or notified by DIAC. *Sources: http://www.environment.gov.au/parks/publications/christmas/pubs/draft-management-plan-p2.pdf and http://www.immi.gov.au/media/publications/pdf/2011/5-roles-and-responsibilities.pdf*
Colombia	Legislated	Has a National System for Evaluation of Management and Results which foxuses on monitoring or results, strategic evaluations and accountability: Colombia's model of evaluation or results management goes beyond a results-based budget. While this is an important element of the model, the system seeks to support the modernization of the Colombian state and to support institutional change, so that our government's human and financial resources become performance oriented. *Sources: http://siteresources.worldbank.org/INTEVACAPDEV/Resources/4585664-1254411557585/colombia_eng.pdf*
Comoros	Plan	There is a poverty reduction and growth strategy for 2010 - 2014. *Source: http://www.imf.org/external/pubs/ft/scr/2010/cr10191.pdf*
Congo, Democratic Republic of the	Plan	USAID is giving assistance to Congo for developing a government performance assessment system. *Source: http://www.countrycompass.com/_docs/assessments/Democratic_Republic_of_the_Congo_Economic_Performance_Assessment.pdf*
Costa Rica	Legislated	Following the United States with their cabinet and agency performance contracts, the Comprimiso de Resultados is only the existence of Performance Management and appraisal systems for cabinet ministers in Costa Rica, where other systems such as financial, procedural and organizational are yet to be adapted through reforms. *Source: http://performance.gov.in/international%20Exe/Costa_20Rica_20Experience.pdf*
Croatia	Plan	Has regular performance evaluations. *Sources: http://www.oecd.org/document/40/0,3746,en_2649_34417_39914600_1_1_1_1,00.html and http://www.oecd.org/dataoecd/2/42/20637229.pdf*
Cuba	Plan	SHRM visited Cuba at the end of last year, Cuban officials said that there is a need for Performance Management to be put in place; also requires performance assessments in healthcare sector. *Sources: http://www.shrm.org/about/news/Pages/DelegationCuba.aspx and http://pmj.bmj.com/content/83/976/105/reply*

Country	Category	Notes
Cyprus	Plan	Performance Management is well and truly active in Cyprus; PwC is in Cyprus, as well as many practitioners, consultants and SMEs. *Sources: http://www.efdergi.hacettepe.edu.tr/english/abstracts/40/pdf/HAKAN%20 ATAMT%C3%9CRK.pdf and http://www.cyprus.com/events/time-and-performance-management-i-info.html*
Czech Republic	Plan	They measure performance in the government via various financial instruments and gathered statistics. *Source: http://iasia-conference2011.org/working-groups/working-group-vi-public-sector-financial-information-and-performance-management/*
Denmark	Legislated	Introduced into the government in 1992, has been refined continuously. A performance pay related system has been introduced to support the regime. *Source: http://www.oecd.org/dataoecd/30/24/2079003.pdf*
Dominican Republic	Plan	USAID is working with the Dominican Republic to help sort out mother-to-child transmission activities. Their Performance Management plan hadn't been updated since 2005. *Source: http://www.usaid.gov/oig/public/fy10rpts/1-517-10-001-s.pdf*
Ecuador	Plan	Through USAID, there has been a Performance Management Plan (PMP) implemented in Ecuador relating to democracy and governance activities; however, the country failed to fulfil guidelines in 2006 and was advised to alter their PMP in 2011. *Sources: http://performance.gov.in/international%20Exe/Costa_20Rica_20Experience.pdf and http://www.usaid.gov/oig/public/fy11rpts/1-518-11-009-p.pdf*
Egypt	Plan	They are trying to reform public employees performance appraisal system after the January revolution. *Source:http://jetems.scholarlinkresearch.org/articles/Reforming%20Government%20 Employees%20Performance%20Appraisal%20System.pdf*
El Salvador	Plan	USAID applying peformance management metrics to maternal and child haelth services. *Source: www.usaid.gov/oig/public/fy11rpts/1-519-11-004-p.pdf*
Estonia	Legislated	Performance Management has been implemented in their government, as documented in a case study. *Source: webh01.ua.ac.be/pubsector/Toulouse/Nomm%20Randma.doc*
Ethiopia	Plan	Ethiopia is adapting and adopting the balanced scorecard model. *Source: http://www.ajol.info/index.php/jbas/article/viewFile/63517/51360*
Falkland Islands (Islas Malvinas)	Plan	Performance indicators are identified in relation to the Islands Plan and departmental Business Plans. *Source: http://www.falklands.gov.fk/documents/The%20Voice,%20Issue%205%20-%20June%20 09%20extra.pdf*
Fiji	Plan	In 2009, re-activiation of Performance Management systems was a priority. *Source: http://fiji.gov.fj/index.php?option=com_content&view=article&id=468:civil-service-reforms&catid=71:press-releases&Itemid=155*
Finland	Legislated	Since 1995, Performance Management has been applied to the whole central government. The idea behind the reform was to emphasize outputs and results instead of inputs and rules and to improve target-setting and follow-up. In this process, performance contracts have played an important role. The contractual model has replaced the old hierarchical, compliance-based guidance and control system. Result negotiations and performance contracts represent decentralised and flexible ways of making government agencies more cost-conscious, responsible and accountable. Performance management has also been considered as one of the main instruments for enhancing strategic thinking and prioritisation among the ministries. *Source: http://www.oecd.org/dataoecd/10/63/1902738.pdf*
France	Plan	There is debate as to whether Performance Management is an electoral or a police issue. *Source: http://policing.oxfordjournals.org/content/2/3/331.abstract*

Country	Category	Notes
Georgia	Legislated	The Performance Management systems in Georgia have mainly been restricted to the local governance level: As part of the 1997 budget reform effort, the city of Szolnok developed performance indicators to evaluate the effectiveness and efficiency of budgetary institutions and various programs for which they were responsible. This analysis gave the Economic Department staff a compelling argument that program budgeting performance data must be taken into account before policy makers make a decision. The City now produces a separate volume to the program budget that identifies performance indicators. This volume not only describes the measurement techniques, but also allows policymakers to understand the expected consequences of their decisions. *Source: www.nispa.org/news/papers/wg2/Mark%20and%20Nayyar.doc*
Germany	Legislated	New Steering Model- a comprehensive Performance Management system that encourages public sector organizations to define their outputs more clearly, place unit managers on performance contracts, and show a customer orientation with more flexible resource allocation and greater reliance placed on outsourcing, contracting-out and privatization. Local authorities, in particular large cities, are most advanced with regard to the implementation of the New Steering Model. They are followed by the Laender. The former and present federal government have recently mplemented some few elements of the New Steering Model. *Source: http://www1.worldbank.org/publicsector/civilservice/rsGermany.pdf*
Ghana	Plan	Performance Management systems are currently in place in Botswana, Ghana, South Africa and Uganda. *Source: http://www.uneca.org/publications/dpmd/public_sector_mangt.pdf*
Ghana	Plan	President Mills To Launch New Performance Management System. *Source: http://www.ghana.gov.gh/index.php/information/press-releases/7579-president-mills-to-launch-new-performance-management-system*
Greece	Plan	No legislated framework for which the Greek government implements Performance Management systems; however, a recent OECD report highlighted the need for Greece to strengthen Performance Management in the areas of public administration and budget. *Source: http://www.oecd.org/dataoecd/6/39/44785912.pdf*
Guernsey	Plan	Guernsey has created a KPI report detailing a cultural strategy for itself for 2011 - 2015. *Sources: http://www.gov.gg/ssp and http://www.gov.gg/CHttpHandler.ashx?id=3405&p=0*
Guyana	Plan	Has economic performance assessments from USAID, but no legislation as yet. *Source: http://www.countrycompass.com/_docs/assessments/Guyana_Economic_Performance_Assessment.pdf*
Hong Kong	Plan	For the Hong Kong Civil Service, Performance Management is a key focus area for them and it is regularly reviewed to make sure that the standard of Performance Management always stays high. *Source: http://www.csb.gov.hk/english/admin/conduct/files/Performance_Mangement-e.pdf*
Hungary	Plan	Whilst there has been no central government initiative to implement Performance Management systems, there have been local government initiatives: "In Hungary, six cities were participating in an overall capacity-building project and all participated in a multi-service citizen survey. Three of the cities – Szolnok, Tatabanya, and Oroshaza – elected to have more intensive assistance in implementing Performance Management in the education sector; they were primarily interested in evaluating citizen satisfaction with current service provision through a direct mail survey of the parents of elementary school students. A fourth city, Szentes, was most interested in the social sector, and formed a working group to assess the effectiveness of the city's services. This effort was carried out in collaboration with an official at the Ministry of Social and Family Affairs, who was interested in identifying ways in which to assess the effect of centrally funded local government social services. *Source: www.nispa.org/news/papers/wg2/Mark%20and%20Nayyar.doc*
Iceland	Plan	Performance Management is implemented in the icelandish economic programme, however it's not legislation. *Source: http://eng.efnahagsraduneyti.is/media/Acrobat/Pre-Accession-Economic-Programme-2011_Iceland.pdf*
India	Plan	Government of India has embarked on a comprehensive reform of the existing Performance Management System. Many interlinked and mutually reinforcing initiatives are being implemented: results-framework document, performance appraisal report, independent evaluation office, PMs delivery monitoring unit, etc. *Source: http://www.performance.gov.in/workshopfolder/1._Vision_to_Action.doc*

Country	Category	Notes
Indonesia	Legislated	Since the Indonesian government determined regulation about regional autonomy in 2002, there were efforts to arrange specific policies for government owned institution in each Indonesian region. Those specific policies also included performance measurement area that the government institutions in local region can manage their own performance report but still have obligation to report their performance condition to central government. That independent Performance Management is based on Undang-Undang Republik Indonesia (Indonesian Regulation) no. 17 / 2003 that applies the implementation refers to the activity area of the government institution activity... There have also been proposals for the implementation of performance management systems in certain areas of government by the ABD. *Sources: http://www.eurojournals.com/ibba_4_05.pdf and http://www2.adb.org/Documents/ RRPS/INO/rrp_ino_32359.pdf*
Iran	Plan	Government management performance systems are minimal in Iran except for a health service contracting one in cooperation with the WHO: In parallel with the development of the industry, measures have been taken to ensure medicine quality, including implementing a performance management system and good manufacturing practices, drawing up a new pharmacopoeia, enforcing a branded generic naming system and establishing a centre for registration and review of adverse drug reactions. *Source: http://www.who.int/countryfocus/cooperation_strategy/ccs_irn_en.pdf*
Iraq	Plan	On September 30, 2009, USAID Iraq and The QED Group, LLC entered an agreement for a monitoring and evaluation program entitled Performance Evaluation and Reporting for Results Management (PERFORM). PERFORM includes monitoring and evaluation services for OFDA and a scope of work is being developed. Following partner specific program reviews, PERFORM will provide field monitoring and reporting and annual or end-of-grant evaluations. *Source: http://www.usaid.gov/oig/public/fy10rpts/e-267-10-001-p.pdf*
Ireland	Plan	Performance Management in the Irish Civil Service-Overview of Performance Management and Development System (PMDS). *Source: http://www.eupan.si/uploads/media/PERFORMANCE_MANAGEMENT_IN_IRISH_CIVIL_ SERVICE_01.pdf*
Isle of Man	Plan	Has Performance Management Systems in multiple departmental areas including the Chief Secretary's Office, Sport Department and internally with its Public Service sector. *Sources: http://www.gov.im/cso/corporate/conduct/performance_management.xml, http:// www.gov.im/sport/SportsDevelopment/Strategy/kpi.xml and http://www.gov.im/lib/docs/hr/ employeedevelopment/governmentwideldstrategy.pdf*
Italy	Plan	Utilizes management performance systems throughout its governmental ministries (esp. balanced scorecard method) and recently, the Presidency of Ministry Council declared Italy's Ministry of Infrastructure and Transportation (MINT) to be the country's first best practice case for management control systems in public administration. *Source: http://www.3ecompass.net/library/view/compass-ibrary/Performance_Management_in_ European_Government.pdf*
Jamaica	Plan	Performance Management Appraisal System (PMAS), which was introduced across the Public Sector in 2006 Cabinet Office: Office of the Prime Minister, Ministry of Finance and Public Service, Ministry of Transport and Works, Office of the Services Commissions, Auditor General's Department, Ministry of Health and Environment, Ministry of Foreign Affairs and Foreign Trade, Ministry of Justice, Ministry of National Security, Ministry of Agriculture and Lands, Auditor General's Department, Post and Telecommunications Department, Department of Correctional Services. Ministry of Tourism and the Institute of Jamaica. *Source: http://www.cabinet.gov.jm/current_initiatives/performance_management_appraisal_ system_pmas*
Japan	Plan	The Road Administration Management approach was begun from FY2003 to promote a shift toward more efficient, effective, and highly transparent road administration. *Source: http://www.mlit.go.jp/road/management-e/index.html*
Jersey	Legislated	Releases annual performance reports in order to evaluate and measure progress of the country in relation to Strategic Plans that the government had drafted years previously. *Source: http://www.gov.je/Government/PlanningPerformance/StrategicPlanning/Pages/ AnnualPerformanceReports.aspx*

Country	Category	Notes
Jordan	Plan	A new regulator for the water sector has yet to be established as recommended by the PPIAF activity. The Performance Management Unit (previously known as the Program Management Unit), housed within the Water Authority of Jordan, remains the regulatory entity overseeing private sector participation projects in the water and sanitation sector in Jordan. *Source: http://www.ppiaf.org/ppiaf/sites/ppiaf.org/files/documents/PPIAF_Assistance_in_Jordan_September_2011.pdf*
Kazakhstan	Plan	Government bodies Performance Management. Initiated by the Public Administration Academy under the President of Kazakhstan, the main purpose of this project is the exchange of good practices and knowledge between the participating countries in the field of Performance Management. Planned starting date: 01/09/2010 Planned end date: 01/02/2011 *Source: http://www.rcpar.org/contents_en.asp?id=369*
Kenya	Legislated	In April 2008, the Coalition Government merged PSR&DS and Performance Contracting Steering Committee (PCSC) to form Public Sector Reforms and Performance Contracting (PSR&PC), under the Office of the Prime Minister. The programme is currently supported by the GoK, the World Bank, UNDP, and the Governments of Canada, Denmark, Finland, Sweden, and the UK. *Source: http://www.psrpc.go.ke/index.php?option=com_content&view=article&id=63:performance-management-a-transformative-leadership&catid=53:departments-psprc&Itemid=101*
Kiribati	Plan	The Government of Kiribati requested ADB to provide technical assistance (TA) to strengthen its economic and financial management systems to better utilize public resources, and to strengthen Government's capacity to conduct sound economic analysis. The primary focus was to assist Kiribati with economic restructuring. It built on progress under an earlier TA (TA 2657-KIR:Strengthening Institutional Capacity for Financial and Economic Management) implemented during 1997–1998. This TA commenced in September 1999 and ran through to end-March 2002. *Source: http://www.adb.org/documents/TACRs/KIR/TACR_KIR_3159.pdf*
Korea, North	Plan	Has an integrated business processing platform while Performance Management, Knowledge Sharing, Information Disclosure, and Process Management are interconnected. *Source: http://www.korea.go.kr/new_eng/service/viewContent.do?enCont Id=00001264605116361000_151*
Korea, South	Plan	The On-nara BPS is a government management system that accommodates document processing and program management online. It was designed in January 2007. *Source: http://unpan1.un.org/intradoc/groups/public/documents/un/unpan031744.pdf*
Kuwait	Plan	State Audit Bureau has received support to develop a Performance Management framework with the Programme Period: 2009/2013. *Source: http://www.undp-kuwait.org/undpkuw/democraticgov/Prodoc_State%20Audit%20Bureau_National%20Performance%20Management%20Framework_13Jan2011SB.pdf*
Laos	Plan	Issued in the governing party's policy reform: Since 2000 we have been in the process of revising our civil service regulations and the Government is now considering the approval of a new Decree on the Civil Service Statute. Through this new statute, the governmentwants to improve efficiency and effectiveness in government, by introducing more performance-oriented human resource management practices... The public service reform program aims to create a merit-based public service and to make the salary structures more competitive and more motivating, while at the same time introducing the practice of regular performance assessments as a basis for Performance Management of both individual employees and organizational units... *Source: http://www.undplao.org/whatwedo/bgresource/demogov/Priority%20Areas%20for%20Gov%20Reform%20PolicyPaper.pdf*
Latvia	Plan	The development of a systematic Performance Management policy-planning system was one of Latvia's goals. But by 2001 this goal remained largely elusive. *Source: http://unpan1.un.org/intradoc/groups/public/documents/nispacee/unpan021457.pdf*
Lebanon	Plan	USAID Performance Management Plan for Lebanon. The MIS/GIS component of the PMPL project begins with a Synergy mission to Lebanon in January 2011. *Source: http://www.synisys.com/index.jsp?sid=3&nid=70&y=2010&m=11&d=6*
Lesotho	Legislated	The government initiated a Performance Management System for the Civil Service of Lesotho but there are no additional details other than a review form. *Source: http://www.mps.gov.ls/documents/Form_PMS_Review.pdf*

Country	Category	Notes
Liberia	Legislated	The Government of Liberia selected FreeBalance Accountability Suite to act as the the GRP system in 2010 after a competitive bid process. The software is to be implemented in five sites with FreeBalance Public Financials Management, Government Performance Management, Public expenditure Management and Civil Service Management functionality. Ministers to Sign Performance Contracts in 2012, the new Performance Management policy requires ministers to sign a one-year renewable contract based on their performance during the year under review. *Source: http://www.freebalance.com/news/2012/LiberiaAwardPR.asp*
Libya	Legislated	There is a government initiated Performance Appraisal System for its public servants which are In accordance with the Libyan Civil Service Act 55/76, which replaced the old Act 19/1964, jobs are divided financially into thirteen grade (1-13). All employees on grades 1-10 irrespective of the nature of their jobs, are subject to annual report (the efficiency report). *Source: http://unpan1.un.org/intradoc/groups/public/documents/cafrad/unpan010159.pdf*
Lithuania	Plan	Lithuania introduced Performance Management in 2000 to bridge the gap between falling budget revenues as a result of a fiscal crisis and increasing governmental commitments owing to its accession to the EU and NATO. *Source: http://www.vpvi.lt/assets/Uploads/towards-results-based-government.pdf*
Macau	Legislated	There is currently a public servant Performance Appraisal System in Macau that also recently underwent improvements to it after a bill was passed by the Legislative Assembly. *Source: http://www.macaucloser.com/older_issues/MacauCLOSER_Site_august_2008/bureaucratic_capacity.html*
Macedonia	Legislated	Ministry of Justice (MOJ) - The leadership and strategic planning skills of the MOJ's top management team have been enhanced, enabling them to align MOJ strategic objectives with those of the Government of Macedonia. In order to monitor and measure the execution of the MOJ strategy, Balanced Scorecards were introduced as a Performance Management system. *Source: http://macedonia.usaid.gov/en/sectors/democracy/HIDP.html*
Madagascar	Plan	USAID/Madagascar agreed to review and update the Health, Population and Nutrition Performance Management plan by the end of calendar year 2011. The plan will include written guidance for calculating couple years of protection and include conversion factors to be used by the mission and implementing partners. *Source: http://www.usaid.gov/oig/public/fy11rpts/4-687-11-012-p.pdf*
Malawi	Legislated	Introduced MTEF to improve the macroeconomic framework which involves Performance Management approaches and tools in 1993. *Source: http://siteresources.worldbank.org/INTPEAM/Resources/malawi.doc*
Malaysia	Legislated	The Performance Management & Delivery Unit (PEMANDU) was formally established on September 16, 2009 and is a unit under the Prime Minister's Department. PEMANDU's main role and objective is to oversee implementation and assess progress of the Economic Transformation Programme and the Government Transformation Programme. Facilitating as well supporting delivery of the national key result area (NKEAs), national key economic areas (NKRAs) and ministerial key result area (MKRAs). *Source: http://www.pemandu.gov.my/*
Malaysia	Plan	The Government today announced six Strategic Reform Initiatives (SRIs), the second critical component of the Economic Transformation Programme (ETP) in addition to the 12 National Key Economic Areas (NKEAs), to boost its global competitiveness. *Source: http://etp.pemandu.gov.my/News_-%E2%97%98-_Events-@-Malaysia_announces_six_Strategic_Reform_Initiatives_to_boost_competitiveness.aspx*
Maldives	Plan	In 1996, the Government of Maldives introduced a performance appraisal system, based on rewarding employees through the assessment of several factors such as quality of work, job knowledge and performance. The reward came in the form of annual salary increments. *Source: http://onlinelibrary.wiley.com/doi/10.1002/pad.189/abstract*
Mali	Plan	It is widely aggreed upon that Mali has few/poor Performance Management systems, however, their Performance indicators were introduced first in certain projects and then, more systematically, in the budget programmes (1998). They are also used in the SWAPs (PRODESS and PRODEC). They are not used, on the contrary, in the preparation of the annual capital budget, or for the Government Budget in general. *Source: http://www.odi.org.uk/resources/docs/2047.pdf*

Country	Category	Notes
Malta	Plan	For all officers in the General Service grades (with the exclusion of officers in the messengerial class), not on a performance agreement, a system of Performance Management has been introduced to measure their effectiveness, productivity and training needs. *Source: http://www.mpo.gov.mt/downloads/psmcrevised.pdf*
Marshall Islands	Plan	The Government has been advised that the availability of Asian Development Fund (ADF) will be determined using a performance-based allocation system. Thus, the level of ADF funds allocated to the RMI is linked to the country's performance with respect to policy, institutional reforms, and portfolio management. Accordingly, the proposed base-case, rolling 3- year allocation is fixed at $10.7 million for 2003-2005. *Source: http://www.adb.org/documents/CSPs/RMI/2002/csp0500.asp?p=doccsps*
Mauritania	Plan	The Mauritania Public Sector Capacity Building Project in March 2012 aims to contribute to improving performance, efficiency, and transparency of public resources management. *Source: http://web.worldbank.org/external/projects/main?Projectid=P082888&theSitePK=40941 &piPK=64290415&pagePK=64283627&menuPK=64282134&Type=Overview*
Mauritius	Plan	The Performance Management System (PMS) which is considered to be a tool to manage and improve performance at all levels in an organisation was formally launched yesterday in the Ministry of Finance and Economic Development by the Deputy Prime Minister and Minister of Finance and Economic Development, Mr. Rama Sithanen, at Sir Harilal Vaghjee Hall. The implementation of the PMS started on a pilot basis in April/May 2006 in three organisations, namely; the Central Statistics Office, the Meteorological Services and the Valuation Department of the Ministry of Finance and Economic Development. On the basis of positive feedbacks from the pilot projects, the PMS was extended to other Ministries/Departments as from January 2007. At present the PMS is being implemented in 19 Ministries/ Departments. *Source: http://www.gov.mu/portal/site/Mainhomepage/menuitem.a42b24128104d9845dabddd15 4508a0c/?content_id=12e19bfab0b16110VgnVCM1000000a04a8c0RCRD*
Mexico	Plan	It was at the end of the 1990s that monitoring and evaluation (M&E) and performance-based management reforms started to take root in the federal public administration. *Source: http://siteresources.worldbank.org/EXTEVACAPDEV/Resources/4585672-1251461875432/ mexico_me_wp20.pdf*
Micronesia, Federated States of Micronesia	Plan	The Asia Bank aided the government of Micronesia in 2000 the implementation of a performance-based budget management system at both state and national level for the country. *Source: http://www2.adb.org/Documents/TARs/FSM/tar_fsm35443.pdf*
Moldova	Plan	Performance Management Plan has been created by USAID with its duration from October 1, 2007 – September 30, 2010. *Source: http://moldova.usaid.gov/sites/default/files/BRTA%20Performance%20Management%20 Plan.pdf*
Mongolia	Legislated	The Government of Mongolia (GoM) introduced a Performance Management system in 2003 as part of the public administration reform. *Source: http://blog-pfm.imf.org/pfmblog/2008/06/strengthening-t.html*
Montserrat	Legislated	The Government of Montserrat through its Public Service Reform Programme has introduced the Performance Management System and began training selected members of government departments to train and assist in the transformation of the service to a performance oriented one in January 2010. *Source: http://www.gov.ms/?p=1911*
Morocco	Plan	There have been a financial Performance Management systems report compiled by the World Bank on Morocco and USAID has advised for Morocco to establish effective Performance Management systems. *Source: https://openknowledge.worldbank.org/handle/10986/3146*
Mozambique	Plan	Performance Management System in the Mozambican Public Service funded by the World Bank and Government of Mozambique with duration from August 2008 (start date) – ongoing. *Source: http://www.ipac.ca/MozambiquePublicSector*
Mozambique	Plan	The Country Program Evaluation (CPE) assessed the overall performance and results of CIDA's interventions in Mozambique from 2004-2005 to 2008-2009, a five-year period corresponding to CIDA's latest Country Development Programming Framework (CDPF) for Mozambique. *Source: http://www.acdi-cida.gc.ca/acdi-cida/ACDI-CIDA.nsf/eng/NAT-78102222-JV2*

Country	Category	Notes
Namibia	Plan	Performance Management System (PMS) for the Public Service of Namibia and Construction of NIPAM Campus with duration from April 2010 to March 2014. *Source: http://www.parliament.gov.na/cms_documents/130_vote_2_prime_minister.pdf*
Nauru	Plan	Regulatory and Governance Reform for Improving Water and Electricity Supply in Nauru along with Technical Assistance (TA) developing a Performance Management system for Nauru Utilities Corporation. *Source: http://pid.adb.org/pid/TaView.htm?projNo=45048&seqNo=01&typeCd=2*
Nepal	Plan	Druing the Bank's Country Program Confirmation Mission in November 1996, the Government requested the Bank for technical assistance (TA) to help introduce/strengthen a results-based project Performance Management system (PPMS) at the national level and within selected line agencies. *Source: http://www.adb.org/Documents/TARs/NEP/31026-NEP-TAR.pdf*
Netherlands	Legislated	In Holland, the importance of teaming up Performance Management and policy evaluation research was first acknowledged in the 1991 government position paper Policy evaluation studies in central government and the following Frame-of-reference for policy evaluation instruments (Ministry of Finance, 1994; updated in 1998). Since the early 1990s, the following categories complementary evaluation instruments are distinguished in the Netherlands Central Government: 1. Systems of performance and effect indicators, which provide periodic insight or monitoring information into government performance and the extent to which policy makers have achieved their aims; 2. (Project-based) policy evaluation research, which usually take place less frequently than once a year and focuses on the net (societal) effects of policy programmes, and 3. Organisational auditing, in which the operational management and performance of specific organisations are reviewed. *Source: http://www.asip.org.ar/en/revistas/45/knaap/knaap_03.php*
New Zealand	Plan	Information on the public sector performance and financial management system with links to Treasury guidance material on this system including the Treasury Instructions and Treasury circulars. *Source: http://www.treasury.govt.nz/publications/guidance*
Niger	Plan	There is a performance appraisal system for the Public Sector of Niger conducted by the Public Administration Department even though it is said to be old and inefficient. *Source: http://ccsenet.org/journal/index.php/ijbm/article/download/10848/7697-h7N8DTew09i2CCQmEC-kNA*
Nigeria	Plan	Installing new Performance Management system of target setting and performance measurement as a basis for evaluating individual and corporate performance. *Source: http://unpan1.un.org/intradoc/groups/public/documents/cafrad/unpan005908.pdf*
Niue	Legislated	Performance Management systems developed and applied at all levels by 2011. *Source: http://www.sprep.org/att/irc/ecopies/countries/niue/40.pdf*
Norfolk Island	Legislated	The Norfolk Island Administration Performance Management System exists which was created in a bill by the House of representatives: The creation of the Performance Management System at Recommendation 11 is seen as the first tangible step towardsfinancial and public sector reform. The 12th Legislative Assemblyhave included in their strategic objectives the continuedimprovement and reform of service delivery by the public sector. *Source: www.aph.gov.au/house/committee/ncet/lawreformbill2010/report/Chapter201.pdf*
Norway	Legislated	The development of Performance Management in the central government administration culminated on 26 January 1996, when the government by royal decree laid down new regulations for financial management in the government administration. The regulations went into force on 10 January 1997, and ministries and subordinate agencies have until 1 July 1998 to make the necessary adjustments. *Source: http://www.oecd.org/dataoecd/11/41/1902765.pdf*

Country	Category	Notes
Pakistan	Plan	Pakistan has also taken initiatives to introduce performance-based remuneration in the government and the public sector. It must be noted here, that private enterprises in Pakistan already have the concept of performance related incentives. As part of reforms in higher education, a Higher Education Commission was created in Pakistan in 2002. The commission focused on a number of initiatives such as sending students abroad on scholarships, building of universities, emphasized on teaching quality and research, targeted plagiarists, etc. With a view to improve teaching quality and research, performance related incentives were introduced by the Commission. The introduction of PRI in the education system has started to yield positive results in terms of enhanced effort being rendered by employees, and improving teaching quality. Similarly, Pakistan's Central Board of Revenue (CBR), has also instituted performance related pay for its employees to create motivation and incentives for better performance. According to published information, the performance of CBR across a range of measures has gone up after instituting performance related incentives and by paying special attention to capacity building, welfare, training etc of its employees. *Source: http://india.gov.in/govt/studies/annex/2.5.3.pdf*
Palau	Legislated	Public sector reform in Palau is guided by the Management Action Plan (MAP). The two areas of focus for the MAP are management and maintenance, which includes improving the work ethic and Performance Management. *Source: http://www.adb.org/Documents/CPSs/PAL/2009/PAL-Public-Sector-Reform.pdf*
Panama	Plan	The Panama government has pledged to implement and improve on its Performance Management systems relating to financial aspects with its government agencies. Create and Support Project Management Capacities: To Provide assistance to MEF, CGR and DGCP in carrying out adequate management, monitoring, reporting, auditing and evaluation of Project implementation activities, as well as to boost Panama's public sector efficiency reform agenda. *Source: http://web.worldbank.org/WBSITE/EXTERNAL/COUNTRIES/LACEXT/PANAMAEXTN /0,,contentMDK:22854331~menuPK:50003484~pagePK:2865066~piPK:2865079~theSite PK:343561,00.html*
Papua New Guinea	Plan	PNGInfo Database System version 2.0 was developed in 2008 and was distributed on CDs. The CDs are offline and can be installed at anyone desk tops available for easy access to data on MDGs and other development indicators which can generate Tables, Maps and Graphs for analysis. Currently PNGInfo v 2.0 is made up of 4 databases last updated in 8/11/2009 namely; PNG MDGs, PNG Human Development Report, PNG MTDS Performance Management Framework and PNG National Censuses. The CDs were distributed during all major workshops like the rolling out of MDGs in the Provinces. *Source: http://www.devinfo.org/Di-wiki/index.php?title=Papua_New_Guinea*
Paraguay	Legislated	Has Performance Management systems for the municipal level of government with the MIDAMOS model: "a set of 31 qualitative and quantitative indicators organised into 5 main themes of municipal management. For each indicator, an evaluation on a 1-5 scale and a relative weight are provided. Municipal performance is then calculated by adding up the weighted value of each indicator score. *Source: http://www.dpwg-lgd.org/cms/upload/pdf/A_users_guide_to_measuring_local_governance. pdf*
Peru	Plan	The European Commission created its own Public Financial Management Performance Report based on PEFA on Peru which had to cooperation of the Peruvian government. *Source: http://ec.europa.eu/europeaid/what/economic-support/public-finance/documents/peru__ pefa_report_en.pdf*
Philippines	Legislated	President Aquino III issued Administrative Order (AO) No. 25 before end-2011, which mandates the development of Results-Based Performance Management System (RBPMS), by integrating the various performance monitoring tools used by oversight agencies, in six months. *Source: http://www.dbm.gov.ph/index.php?pid=3&nid=2448*
Pitcairn Islands	Legislated	The GPI Performance Management system (PMS) focuses on the overall performance of the Government of Pitcairn Islands, its specific divisions, its employees and processes and aims to significantly improve performance. *Source: http://www.government.pn/policies/GPI%20010%20GPI%20Performance%20 Management%20Policy.pdf*

Country	Category	Notes
Poland	Plan	Management systems being introduced for labor market programs in Poland are examples of performance driven government. They are idealized versions of systems like those called for by the Government Performance and Results Act of 1993 passed by the 103rd United States Congress. 1 In Poland, performance indicators have been specified to measure the success of each labor market program... In Poland the system for Performance Management of active labor programs is being implemented under World Bank project Terms of Reference 2 (TOR 2). Goals for labor programs were stated by TOR 2 Advisory and Steering Committees in March of 1993. *Source: http://research.upjohn.org/cgi/viewcontent.cgi?article=1054&context=confpapers*
Portugal	Plan	In Portugal, the revision of the performance appraisal system is particularly necessary, since the new reform framework of attachments/links, careers and remunerations shall come into force at the beginning of 2008. In France, a report of the committee sur le coût et le rendement des services publics (2006) recommended continuing with the reform of the appraisal system and in particular to further developed the instrument of target agreements. *Source: http://www.dgaep.gov.pt/media/0601010000/alemanha/performance%20assessment.pdf*
Qatar	Plan	To build a strong foundation, two programmes must start during the planning phase: expanding the support of central government functions and developing a public sector Performance Management framework. *Source: http://www2.gsdp.gov.qa/www1_docs/NDS_EN.pdf*
Romania	Plan	The process of reorganizing the internal control system is complex and has deep implication starting with the definition and understanding of the internal control concept in the Anglo-Saxon acceptation approved by the European Union, the reorganization of the internal control systems in the sense of dissipating the control and inspection activities within the process fluxes within entities and implementing the internal control standards stipulated by the Order of the Ministry of Public Finances no. 946/2005 in Romania. Practically, the implementation of the new managerial control system represents, also, a problem related to the organizational culture within the field in Romania. Within this revolutionary process for the reorganization of the internal control and management system, the entities are confronted with the necessity of setting up working groups that will monitor the process of implementing the managerial control system, with the necessity of setting up a Risk Register and, finally, with the necessity of elaborating operational working procedures for each activity that contributes at the realization of the public entity's objectives. *Source: http://incda-fundulea.ro/rar/nr25/rar25.17.pdf*
Russia	N/A	There is at present no effective system for Performance Management in place for goverment. *Source: http://www.imf.org/external/pubs/ft/seminar/2000/invest/pdf/parison.pdf*
Rwanda	Plan	With the aid of Western nations, Rwanda has undertaken 'Performance Based Financing' in its Health Sector in 2001: "Performance based financing, or "pay-4-performance" or "output based aid" as it is generally referred to, consists of a family of various methods and approaches that all aim, through differing levels of intervention, at linking incentives to performance. *Source: http://www.mfdr.org/sourcebook/2ndEdition/4-3RwandaPBF.pdf*
Saint Helena	Plan	Value for Money audits are conducted by the Audit Service on behalf of the Legislative Council, inorder to determine whether St Helena Government resources have been used with proper regard toeconomy, efficiency and effectiveness. *Source: http://www.audit.gov.sh/publications/vfm_performance_indicators_pwd_final.pdf*
Saint Kitts and Nevis	Plan	Whilst there is no current Performance Management system, an address last year illustrated a need for one: Mr. Speaker, the Office of the Prime Minister has been allocated $12,919,442 for 2011 to carry out its various programmes and activities... The main objective is to improve the efficiency and responsiveness of the Public Service. In addition, the Human Resource Management Department will be using the information from a job evaluation exercise to develop standardized job descriptions for the personnel in all Ministries. Technical assistance would be sought to develop and implement a Performance Management System. *Source: http://www.cuopm.com/pdf/Budget_Addresses/2011_Budget_Address_20101214.pdf*
Saint Lucia	Plan	Problems with their own management performance systems have been identified - No appraisal of top management, Insufficient emphasis placed upon the performance appraisal system, No uniformity in standards set for performance. *Source: http://www.stlucia.gov.lc/docs/Publicsectorreformwhitepaper.pdf*

Country	Category	Notes
Saint Vincent and the Grenadines	Plan	Phase IV of the reform process began in 2000 with a diagnostic review of the performance appraisal system with a view to implementing a new Performance Management system. The new Performance Management system was viewed as highly objective, transparent, continuous and results oriented. The system was also capable of succession and career planning. One of the key reforms initiated by the Public Sector Reform Unit (PSRU) was the implementation of the Performance Management Development System (PMDS). In 2000 a review of the then existing performance appraisal process was conducted and it discovered that the system was largely subjective, lacked continuity, was not transparent and was not linked to ministerial /departmental strategic objectives. *Source: http://www.caricad.net/UserFiles/File/casestudysvg.pdf*
Samoa	Plan	The Human Resource Management Services Unit provides advice to the Commission, line Ministries and other stakeholders on Human Resource policies, monitor and evaluate their effective implementation in Ministries and institute a value based Samoa Public Service - namely one of its functions being overseeing Performance Management. *Source: http://www.psc.gov.ws/hr_management.htm*
Saudi Arabia	Legislated	Recently, the Saudi Performance Measurement Center for Government Agencies (PMCGA) was created in order to institutionalize and monitor Performance Measurement practices across government agencies in the Kingdom of Saudi Arabia which used QPR as its system. Additionally, the Saudi Arabia Kingdom agreed to use QPR Metrics as an electronic system to document, communicate, measure, track and manage all strategic and operational objectives along with their KPIs for the Training Sector of the government owned Saline Water Conversion Corporation. *Sources: http://www.qpr.com/Default.aspx.LocID-00pnew031.RefLocID-00p02200500l.Lang-EN.htm and http://www.qpr.com/Default.aspx.LocID-00pnew02q.RefLocID-00p02200500l.Lang-EN.htm*
Senegal	Plan	The Senegal government and USAID work closely to create and monitor Performance Management Plans in areas of health and agriculture: The USAID/Senegal EG Office tracks GFSR indicators as part of the program's Performance Management Plan (PMP) and the annual Performance Plan and Report (PPR). *Sources: http://feedthefuture.gov/sites/default/files/country/strategies/files/FTF_2010_Implementation_Plan_Senegal.pdf and http://pdf.usaid.gov/pdf_docs/PNADC730.pdf*
Serbia and Montenegro	Plan	Serbia Performance Management Programme conducted with the European Commission in order to have performance improvement in 2 local government services in pilot LAs as a result of a systematic use of performance indicators. A systematic approach to Performance Management is adopted in pilot LAs within the SCTM framework. *Source: http://www.jp.coe.int/CEAD/JP/Default.asp?ID=23324*
Seychelles	Legislated	Seychelles has legislated the use of Performance Appraisal Systems in two areas with the Gender Management System (GMS) in order to ensure gender equality and Performance Appraisal System for Teachers which was introduced in January 2011. *Sources: http://www.uneca.org/acgs/beijingplus15/Questionnaire/DAW/English/Seychelles%20Response%20to%20DAW%20Questionnaire.pdf and http://planipolis.iiep.unesco.org/upload/Seychelles/Seychelles_Education_Reform_Action_Plan_2009-2010.pdf*
Sierra Leone	Plan	Njala University (NU) and Eastern Polytechnic have finally joined the University of Sierra Leone (USL) to embrace the novel administrative policy of the signing of Performance Management contracts by public servants. Performance Contract is a freely negotiated performance agreement between government as the owner of an agency and the management of the institution. Tools such as responsibilities and expectations among both parties enable them achieved their set goals. *Source: http://www.statehouse.gov.sl/index.php?option=com_content&view=article&id=463:njala-eastern-polytechnic-embrace-pmc&catid=34:news-articles*
Singapore	Legislated	Performance Management approaches in Singapore include a performance-informed budgeting system, a performance pay system, and organizational quality assurance strategies such as ISO certifications. *Source: http://www.instituteforgovernment.org.uk/pdfs/casestudy_singapore.pdf*
Solomon Islands	Plan	A Performance Management system is to be developed, incorporating individual appraisals of performance against key competencies. It is intended that Provincial Police Commanders and other key managers will roll out this new system in their work units from 2010. *Source: http://www.ausaid.gov.au/publications/pdf/appr-08-solomon-islands.pdf*

Country	Category	Notes
South Africa	Legislated	Legislated Medium Term Strategic Framework in order to improve government performance so that they can measure outcomes and monitor the supporting chain of inputs-activities outputs, then they will get the fullest attention. Scarce resources and management time will be allocated to them... there is also a Minister for Performance Management Monitoring and Evaluation who oversees this program. *Source:http://www.info.gov.za/view/DownloadFileAction?id=106599*
South Africa	Plan	Performance Management systems are currently in place in Botswana, Ghana, South Africa and Uganda. *Source: http://www.uneca.org/publications/dpmd/public_sector_mangt.pdf*
Spain	Plan	Component II includes the addition of an epidemiologist to provide assistance to local health departments, the establishment of a joint data center with the UNMC College of Public Health, the creation of a Policy Training Academy, a project to conduct Return on Investment studies, the creation of a cardiovascular disease syndromic surveillance system, and assistance to local health departments for accreditation and establishing Performance Management systems. *Source: http://mchdata.hrsa.gov/TVISReports/Documents/2012/Narratives/NE-Narratives.pdf*
Sri Lanka	Plan	To date, studies on measuring health sector performance, have had little impact on developing country health systems and have been limited to explorations primarily at an operational level. However, there is a growing recognition that there is a need to strengthen the policy function of ministries and their ability to monitor policy impact. Sri Lanka is one country that has identified the need to strengthen policy at national level. Many developing countries, like Sri Lanka, are familiar with input, process and output dimensions of operational performance. However, most are not ready to engage in routine performance assessment that can strengthen policy processes at national level. *Source: http://www.ncbi.nlm.nih.gov/pubmed/12126211*
Sudan (South)	Plan	The civil service recruitment system is being revised to ensure that it fully meets government needs, and a Performance Management system is being introduced. *Source: http://www.jdt-juba.org/wp-content/uploads/2012/02/South-Sudan-Development-Plan-2011-13.pdf*
Swaziland	Legislated	Has established a Management Services Division under the Ministry of Public Service with an aim to establish a robust Performance Management System and ensure it is effectively utilized for the Swaziland Civil Service. *Source: http://www.gov.sz/index.php?option=com_content&view=article&id=382&Itemid=390*
Sweden	Legislated	Management by performance began in Sweden's public administration in the late 1980s, both as a tool for the government's budget process and as a way for the government to control its agencies. This article discusses various aspects of the performance system in the Swedish context.
Switzerland	Plan	Performance and Reward Link (PRI) has been largely put in place by most of the OECD countries for the government sector. Different countries have also adopted different methodologies for introducing PRI, ranging from introduction by the central government to consultative mechanisms instituted at the organizational level. For example, PRI was introduced by law in Germany, Hungary, Italy, Spain, Switzerland, USA whereas PRI was introduced by collective agreement in Denmark, Finland and Sweden. Merit increments: from 4.1-6% for outstanding performance (ranked A++). Increase of 3% if assessment is A (good performance). Bonuses can reach 12% of salary for outstanding performance. If bad performance, no bonus and after two years decrease of the salary to 94% in the range of the salary. (Source: OECD (2005) Performance Related Pay Policies for Government Employees, OECD Publishing.). *Source: http://india.gov.in/govt/studies/annex/2.5.3.pdf*
Taiwan	Plan	It is anticipated that this sharing of experience and exchanging of ideas between domestic and overseas experts with regard to e-governance Performance Management will facilitate future planning and implementation of e-governance initiatives in Taiwan. *Source: http://www.rdec.gov.tw/ct.asp?xItem=4535461&ctNode=14650&mp=110* Being in charge of establishing and promoting government Performance Management system, the RDEC has developed: (1) a three level system for monitoring and evaluating program implementation; (2) a government performance evaluation system, and (3) a national corporation performance evaluation system (See Chart 7 and 8), which are designed to monitor the progress of policy implementation and evaluate the performances of government agencies and national government-run corporations. *Source: http://www.rdec.gov.tw/ct.asp?xItem=4088059&ctNode=14537&mp=110*

Country	Category	Notes
Tanzania	Plan	The first phase spanning the year 2000 to June 2007 adapted the theme Instituting Performance Management Systems. The second phase whose implementation commenced in July 2007 is expected to run until June 2012, and it flies under the banner of Enhanced performance and Accountability". The third phase is envisioned to operate from July 2012 to June 2017; its thrust set to be "Quality Improvement Cycle. The implementation process of the PSRP is spearheaded by the President's Office-Public Service Management (PO-PSM). *Source: http://www.capam.org/_documents/bana.benson.paper.pdf*
Thailand	Legislated	In accordance with the State Administration Act of 2002, the Office of the Public Sector Development Commission (OPDC) was established and given the responsibility for introducing changes to improve public management and promoting continuing high performance of Thai public agencies at both national and provincial levels. In 2003, OPDC implemented the results-based management (RBM) approach to measure and drive performance of the Royal Thai ministries, departments and 75 provincial administrations. In fiscal year 2004, all government agencies were required by the Cabinet to join in the system of the performance agreement and measurement from which a series of key performance indicators were used to set target goals. *Source: http://siteresources.worldbank.org/INTTHAILAND/Resources/ CDP-G/392030-1163054967445/Jeanne_Marie_Results_based_management_in_Thailand.pdf*
Timor-Leste	Legislated	Utilizes performance dashboards for performance indication and releases these results to the public in areas of budget, aid, electronic procurement and results of government. *Source: http://www.transparency.gov.tl/*
Togo	Plan	The Bank of African Development has in cooperation with Togo analysed the Key Performance Indicators of Togolese Public Finance Management. *Source: http://www.afdb.org/fileadmin/uploads/afdb/Documents/Project-and-Operations/AR_ to%20En.pdf*
Tokelau	Plan	Tokelau National Strategic Plan (1July 2010 – 30 June 2015) - Improved governance, public sector and financial management, taxation and revenue administration: Percentage of departments and villages implement effectively Staff Performance Management and Review processes. *Source: http://www.tokelau.org.nz/Strategic+Plan.html*
Tonga	Legislated	Has established the Public Service Commission as a government department in order to c) set standards for performance and manage any Performance Management system for the Public Service. *Source: http://www.mic.gov.to/ministrydepartment/govt-departments/public-enterprises*
Trinidad and Tobago	Plan	Developed country status by the year 2020 is the guiding vision and mandate of the Government of Trinidad and Tobago. Therefore, attempts to implement an integrated Performance Management system across the public service is seen as critical in achieving superior organizational performance towards the enhancement and delivery of quality public services. *Source:http://unpan1.un.org/intradoc/groups/public/documents/caricad/unpan017179.pdf*
Tunisia	Plan	Yet to be implemented, however their plans relating to HRM restructuring relate to: establishing Performance Management instruments that emphasise performance appraisal and merit-based pay. *Source: http://www.oecd.org/document/5/0,3746, en_34645207_34645555_45695557_1_1_1_1,00.html*
Turkey	Plan	Quality Development and Performance Assesment Impelmentaion in Hospitals. *Source: http://www.performans.saglik.gov.tr/content/files/yayinlar_yeni/quality_development_ and_performance_assessment_implementation_in_hospitals.pdf*
Turkmenistan	Plan	The European Commission has flagged the transformation of Turkmenistan from a centrally-planned to a market-orientated system with one of the results being the developing of key indicators on performance budgeting (strategy, performance measures and targets) and Performance Management (reporting result, verification and monitoring, programme evaluation). *Source: http://ec.europa.eu/europeaid/documents/aap/2011/af_aap_2011_tkm.pdf*
Tuvalu	Plan	In a report by the Pacific Islands Forum Secretariat, the government is encouraged to initiate the implementation of a Performance Management system as planned in TK II. *Source: http://www.forumsec.org.fj/resources/uploads/attachments/documents/2011_Peer_ Review_Tuvalu_Report.pdf*

Country	Category	Notes
Uganda	Legislated	Result Oriented Management (ROM) and Output Oriented Budgeting (OOB)... The implementation of Results Oriented Management (ROM) in the public service has been a policy objective of Government for several years. ROM is closely linked to OOB and has similar aims, but ROM operates at a lower institutional level than OOB. Results Oriented Management aims to measure achievement at the institutional, departmental and individual level... Also, IDAMC (internally delegated area management contracts) is used by the Mnistry of Water and Environment with five KPI's cascaded to the areas are: NRW, Cash operating margin, Reduction in arrears, Connection efficiency (%age of active accounts) and working ratio. *Sources: http://www.opm.go.ug/ and http://www.oecd.org/dataoecd/50/55/33670399.pdf*
Uganda	Plan	Performance Management systems are currently in place in Botswana, Ghana, South Africa and Uganda. *Source: http://www.uneca.org/publications/dpmd/public_sector_mangt.pdf*
Ukraine	Plan	This report summarizes the findings and recommendations from an evaluation of CIDA's Ukrain Country Program conducted by the Evaluation Division of the Performance and Knowledge Management Branch (PKMB), as part of its 2004 work-plan. The Ukrain Program is a non-typical program in the sense that it has the investments in the traditional CIDA areas of Govenance, Private Sector and Economic Development henceforce referred to regular Program and the non-traditional areas of Nuclear Safety and Non Proliferation. *Source: http://www.acdi-cida.gc.ca/INET/IMAGES.NSF/vLUImages/Internal%20Audits/$file/Ukraine%20Country%20-%20Program%20Evaluation.pdf*
United Arab Emirates	Legislated	Dubai Crown Prince has adopted a Performance Management System for Dubai government employees. *Source: http://www.ameinfo.com/160742.html*
United Arab Emirates	Plan	The United Arab Emirates federal government wanted to deliver an improvement plan for public services aimed at reaching strategic targets by the end of 2010. The key to delivery of the transformation strategy is an automated Performance Management system, called ADAA (performance in Arabic), based on Microsoft® Office PerformancePoint® Server 2007 business intelligence software. Every quarter, federal government entities submit their progress reports to the Prime Minister's Office, which then uses automated tools to measure their performance based on more than 3,000 key performance indicators. *Source: http://www.microsoft.com/casestudies/ServeFileResource.aspx?4000008448-WQL34BaK6J0fYw*
United Kingdom	Legislated	Performance measuring and management in the British public service has become almost ubiquitous over the past three decades. With the exception of some regional government controlled services, virtually every part of the UK public services produces publicly available performance data which has rogressively started to play a role in central decision making. Considerable capacity to formulate, monitor and analyse performance information has evolved. The UK has been successful in developing a fairly comprehensive performance and evaluation measurement, monitoring, and management system which, over time, has become increasingly outcome focussed, although at various levels it still includes large elements of output, process and even input monitoring. The British Performance Management model has largely been a centralized, top-down, imposed one in which lower tier organizations are mandated - either legally or administratively - to produce performance reporting data. The Public Service Agreements System (PSAs) have come to be seen as the international model par excellence of the setting of performance targets broadly linked to the budget process and, therefore, as the pinnacle of the whole system. *Source: http://siteresources.worldbank.org/INTEVACAPDEV/Resources/ecd_24.pdf*
United States	Legislated	One strength of the US federal government, for which it has a global reputation, is its transparency. A recent key initiative is the introduction of online dashboards, an example of the federal sector employing a proven private sector management tool. The dashboards, proposed in the eGov Act of 2002, are hosted on the web, allowing all stakeholders to review the expenditure and activities of various federal agencies. Current dashboards include: • CMS Early Warning System: tracks the effectiveness of Medicare fraud prevention efforts. • USAspending.gov – how the government spends tax dollars. • RegInfo.gov – tracks proposed agency rules through the rulemaking process. • IT Dashboard – monitors IT investments across the federal government. • Recovery.gov – tracks the spending of money allocated in the Reinvestment Act of 2009. • Foreign Assistance –examines US Government foreign assistance spending. *Source: http://www.cgma.org/Resources/Reports/DownloadableDocuments/strategic-performance-public-sector.pdf*

Country	Category	Notes
Uruguay	Legislated	Results-Based Management Evaluation System (SEV) along with a Reformed Constitution of 1967 where the OPP was created which introduced program budgeting, and mandated the Executive to submit Accountability Reports and Budget Execution Reports to Congress. Various decrees were also enacted which include: Decree 104 (1968): Entrusted OPP with the evaluation of compliance of public agencies' compliance with their objectives and budgetary targets; Decree 140 (1995): created CEPRE, which was put in charge of conceptualizing and designing SEV; Decree 255 (1995): Established that the budget cycle must be clearly linked to the programs' intended results, and mandated the introduction of results-based management; National Budget Law of 1995-1999: mandated CEPRE to set up a budgetary evaluation system, and agencies to provide OPP with the information that it requires. *Source: http://siteresources.worldbank.org/INTEVACAPDEV/Resources/4585664-1254408803979/experience_inst_lac.pdf*
Vanuatu	Plan	The government does not have a system itself, however, its Public Finance Managements were recently assessed in 2006 using the Public Expenditure and Financial Accountability Performance Management system by the European Commission. *Source: http://ec.europa.eu/europeaid/what/economic-support/public-finance/documents/vanuatu_pefa_en.pdf*
Vietnam	Legislated	Strengthening of Elements of the Position-Based Career System in Vietnam has been discussed with criticism about the Law on Public Officials and Civil Servants which include language regarding the evaluation of individual civil servants' performance but lacks a clear merit base and is not tailored to the specific nature and responsibilities of each position. More thought needs to be given to how the current PM system can be reformed to better meet the needs and tasks of each position. *Source: http://wws.princeton.edu/research/pwreports_f08/WWS591b.pdf*
Virgin Islands	Plan	Government of the British Virgin Islands-Performance Management-User Handbook. Wherever we work, in whatever department, we have a key role to play in helping the BVI Government achieve its objectives. Enabling and motivating everyone to play their part effectively is the purpose of managing performance. *Source: http://www.hr.gov.vg/upload/Performance%20Management%20Handbook.pdf*
West Bank	Plan	Performance Management plans authorized by the government and USAID by implementer of the aid. *Source: http://www.usaid.gov/oig/public/fy12rpts/6-294-12-003-p.pdf*
Zambia	Legislated	The Government of Zambia has put in place the Performance Management package which, among other things, measures the individual performance of officers. *Source: http://www.governance.gov.zm/downloads/CSAR.pdf*
Zimbabwe	Plan	The first phase of the Zimbabwean Civil Service Performance Management Programme was introduced in 1992. Phase Two began in 1997/8 with every civil servant involved. Today there is still talk on Performance Management, now in its fourth phase christened Result Based Management, but there is nothing serious except confusing people and diverting their attention from the problems they are experiencing because of the economic turmoil. Source: http://www.workinfo.com/articles/improving_performance_zim.htm The Zimbabwe Intergrated Performance Management Solution (ZIPMAS) is also a consolidated electronic system used within Government of Zimbabwe for reporting, evaluating and processing financial transactions and staff appraisals. *Source: http://www.gisp.gov.zw/index.php?option=com_content&view=article&id=60&Itemid=56*

Trends in Search

The popularity of Performance Management at all levels was analysed using Google AdWords, based on specific keywords. The Global Monthly Searches statistics in the Table 1 provide the approximate 12-month average of user queries for each keyword on Google Search (Google AdWords 2012).

Figure 1 shows that the keyword search of "Balanced Scorecard" on Google has been experiencing an overall downward turn with seasonal fluctuations. The volume of news reference was relatively stable over time, with a few sharp increases and decreases.

Comparing the first five keywords, it is clear that "Balanced Scorecard" shows the most extreme but still coherent pattern. "Performance Management" and "Strategy Management" show the pattern of decreasing search volume and increasing news references, illustrating a symbiotic relationship. Active search does not have to be undertaken any longer since media already covers this field of interest. Even so, this still does not explain the decrease in search volume, especially for the first four years.

Regarding Figure 2: Trends on Google for "BI" for the years 2004-2011, it has to be noted that BI (or "bi") has everyday meanings in other languages. Still, the trend direction should not be influenced very much by this, since the use of BI in other contexts is likely to be stable.

As shown in Figure 2, the popularity based on search volume for "BI" remained stable between 2004 and 2006. From 2007, there was a steady upward trend. In terms of news references, little to no references were recorded between 2004 and 2007, however from the 4th quarter of 2008, the term BI gained a sharp rise in news coverage and has remained relatively stable since.

Summarising the trends of the first five key terms, one has to acknowledge that there is not an overall trend. In fact, whereas "BI" and "Analytics" experienced a steep increase, while in the case of "Metrics" it was quite the opposite. The mostly stable trends for "Scorecard" and "Dashboard" only slumped during the GFC.

No.	Keyword	Global Monthly Searches
1	Balanced Scorecard	550,000
2	Performance Management	450,000
3	Strategy Management	246,000
4	Strategy Implementation	60,500
5	Performance Management System	60,500
6	Strategy Execution	14,800
7	Business Performance Management	14,800
8	Corporate Performance Management	12,100
9	Strategic Performance Management	6,600
10	Enterprise Performance Management	6,600

Table 1: Search volume for Performance Management - Organizational level keywords

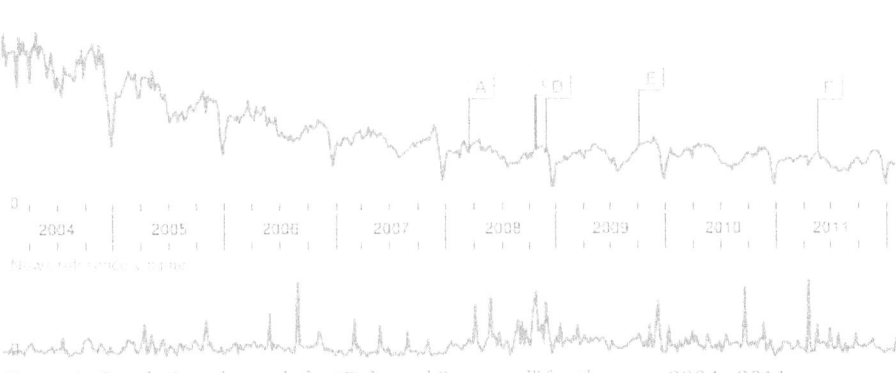

Figure 1: Google Search trends for "Balanced Scorecard" for the years 2004 - 2011.

No.	Keyword	Global Monthly Searches
1	BI	30,400,000
2	Analytics	7,480,000
3	Dashboard	4,090,000
4	Metrics	4,090,000
5	Scorecard	1,500,000
6	KPI	832,000
7	Business Intelligence	823,000
8	Key Performance Indicators	201,000
9	Performance Measures	135,000
10	Operational Performance Management	1,600

Table 2: Searche volume for Performance Management - Operational level keywords

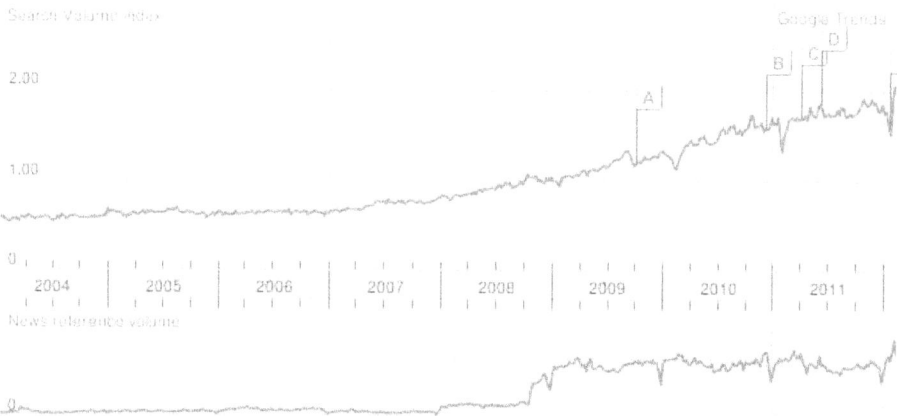

Figure 2: Google Search trends for "BI" between 2004-2011. BI (or "bi") has everyday meanings in other languages.

There has been a relative constant news coverage for the term "Performance Appraisal". However, in 2004, the keyword "Performance Appraisal" had the highest search volume compared to all consecutive years. One reason could be that "Performance Appraisal" is used by individuals nowadays, but may have not been as clearly defined and thus used more broadly in the past.

There is not enough data to build a single, strong argument for this pattern. Instead, it seems to be the case of a composite trend, made out of increased accuracy of definitions. Also, there is a shift from the usage of the term "performance" at the personal level. ■

No.	Keyword	Global Monthly Searches
1	Performance Appraisal	550,000
2	Performance Review	450,000
3	Performance Evaluation	301,000
4	Performance Criteria	165,000
5	Employee Performance	135,000
6	Personal Development Plan	49,500
7	Employee Performance Management	9,900
8	Performance Management Plan	5,400
9	Individual Performance Plan	1,900
10	Individual Performance Management	1,300

Table 3: Search volumes for Performance Management - Individual level keywords

Figure 3: Google Search trends for "Performance Appraisal" between 2004-2011

Organizational Performance Management

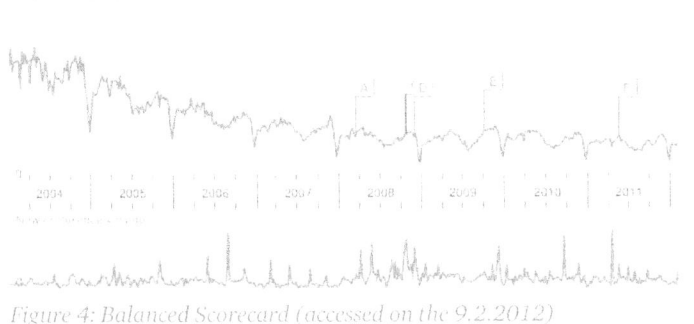

Figure 4: Balanced Scorecard (accessed on the 9.2.2012)

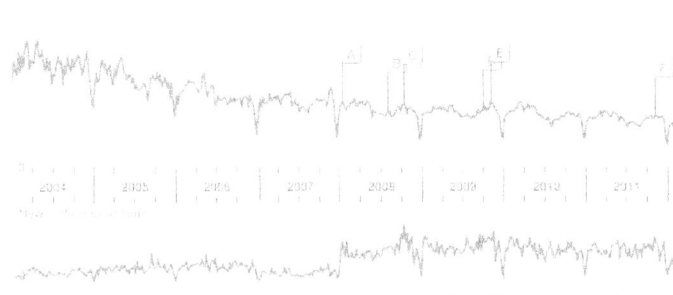

Figure 5: Performance Management (accessed on the 9.2.2012)

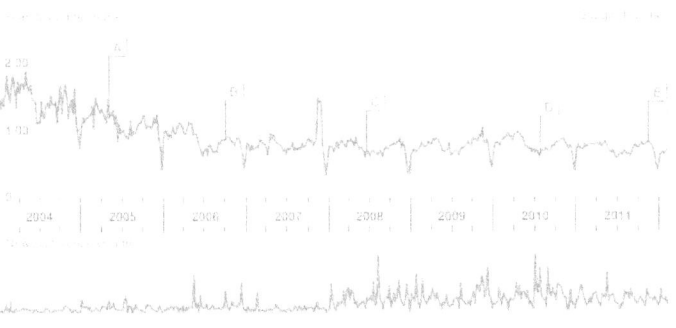

Figure 6: Strategy Management (accessed on the 9.2.2012)

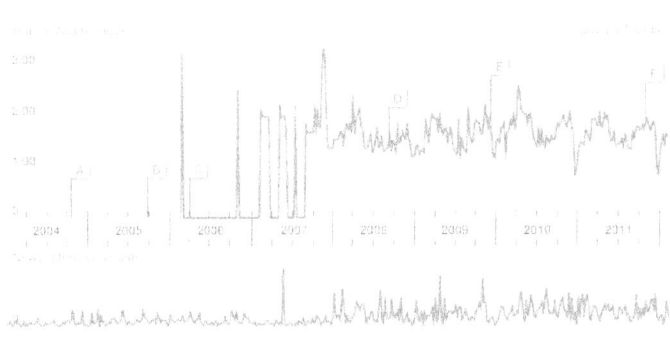

Figure 7: Strategy Implementation (accessed on the 9.2.2012)

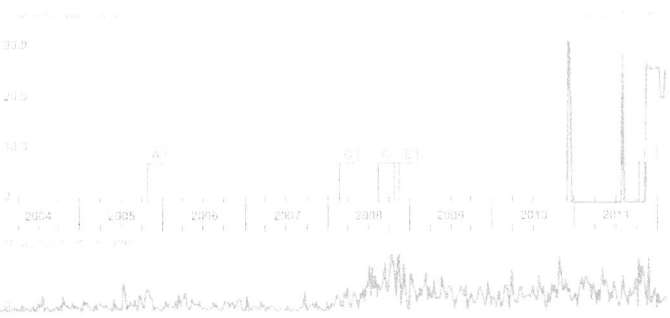

Figure 8: Strategy Execution (accessed on the 9.2.2012)

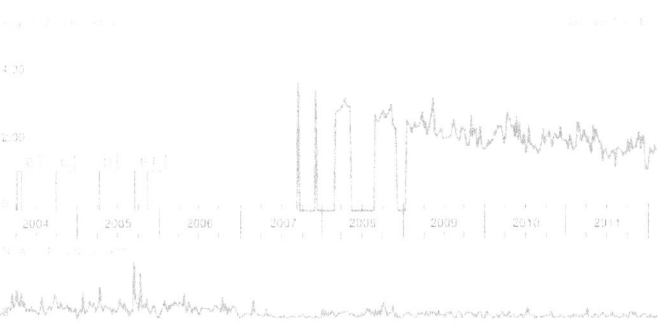

Figure 9: Business Performance Management (accessed on the 9.2.2012)

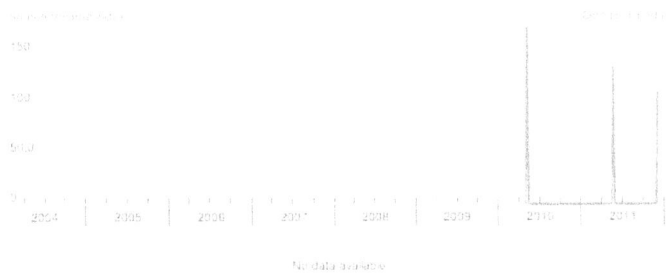

Figure 10: Strategic Performance Management (accessed on the 9.2.2012)

"All good strategy eventually degenerates into work."
Peter Drucker

Operational Performance Management

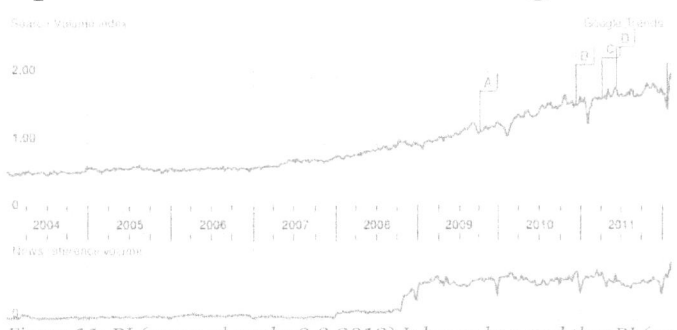

Figure 11: BI (accessed on the 9.2.2012) It has to be noted that BI (or "bi") has everyday meanings in other languages.

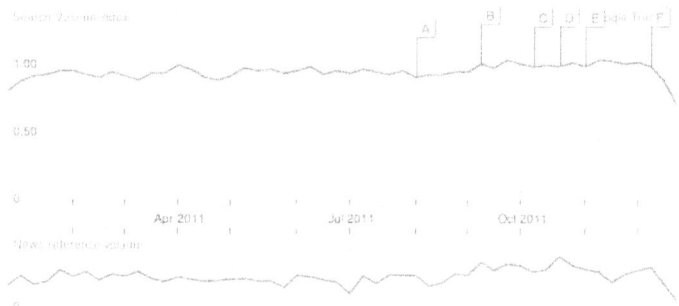

Figure 12: Analytics (accessed on the 9.2.2012)

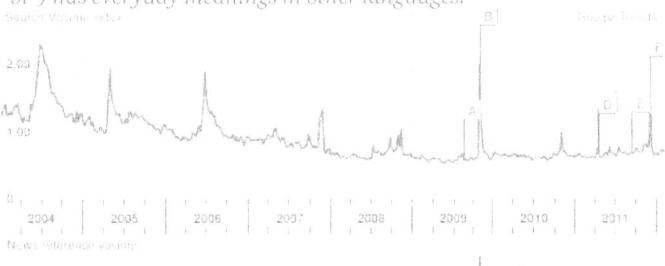

Figure 13: Dashboard (accessed on the 9.2.2012)

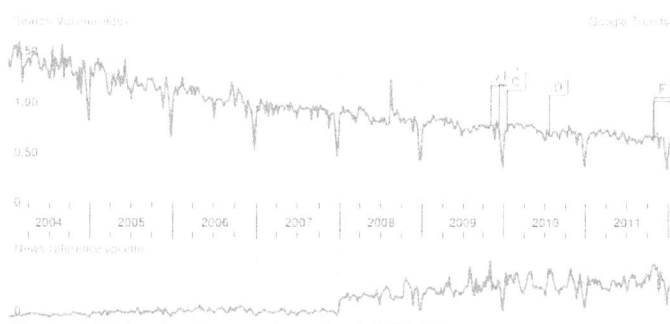

Figure 14: Metrics (accessed on the 9.2.2012)

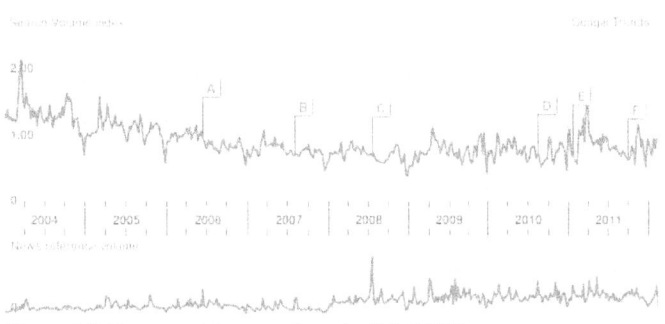

Figure 15: Scorecard (accessed on the 9.2.2012)

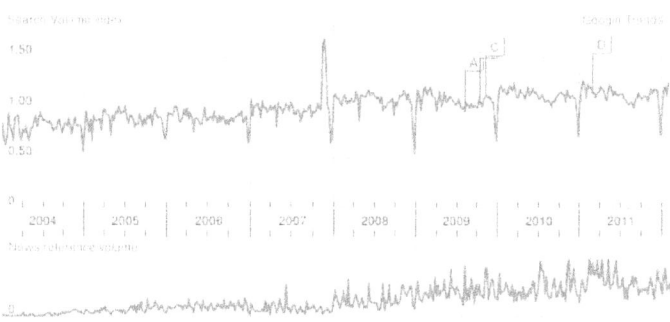

Figure 16: KPI (accessed on the 9.2.2012)

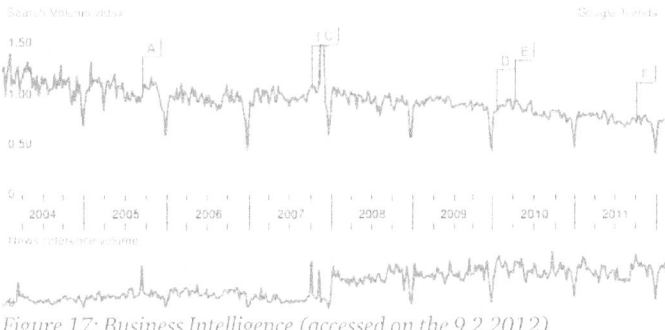

Figure 17: Business Intelligence (accessed on the 9.2.2012)

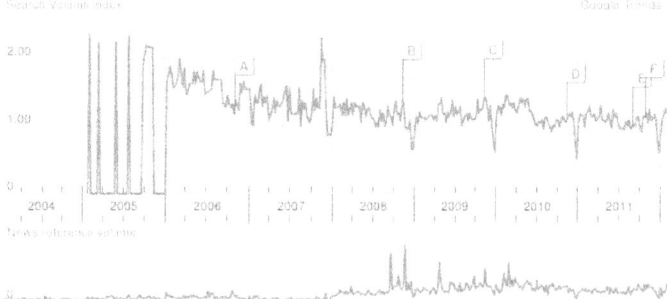

Figure 18: Key Performance Management (accessed on the 9.2.2012)

> *"Accuracy and clarity of statement are mutually exclusive."*
> *Niels Bohr*

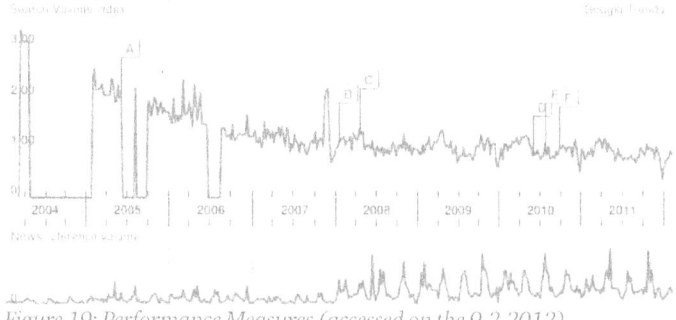

Figure 19: Performance Measures (accessed on the 9.2.2012)

Individual Performance Management

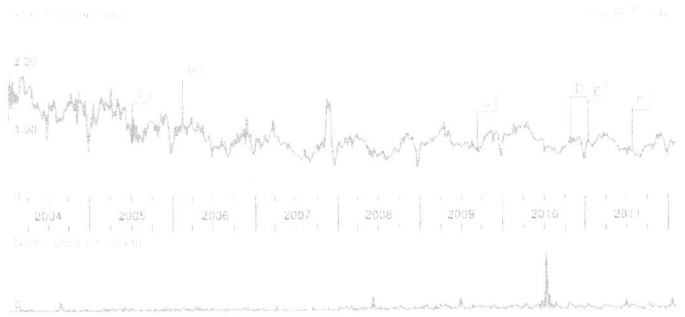

Figure 20: Performance Appraisal (accessed on the 9.2.2012)

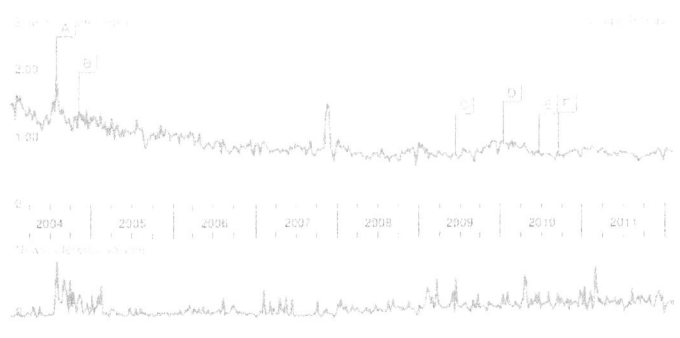

Figure 21: Performance Review (accessed on the 9.2.2012)

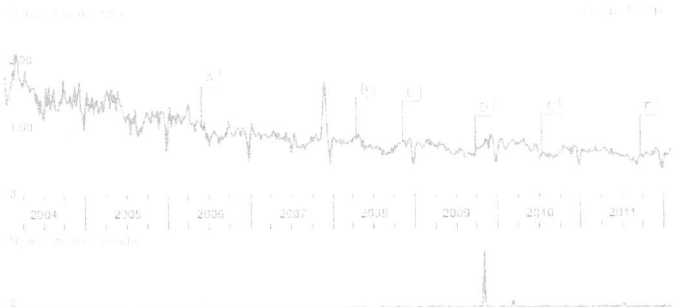

Figure 22: Performance Evaluation (accessed on the 9.2.2012)

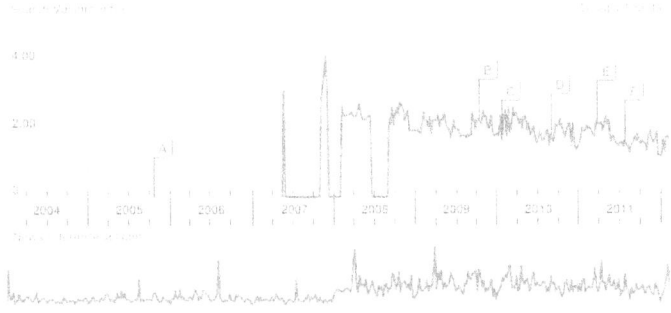

Figure 23: Performance Criteria (accessed on the 9.2.2012)

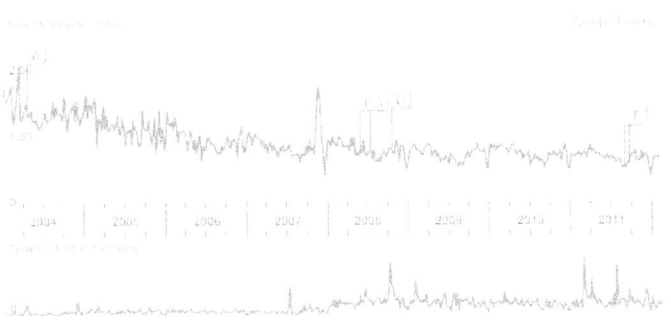

Figure 24: Employee Performance (accessed on the 9.2.2012)

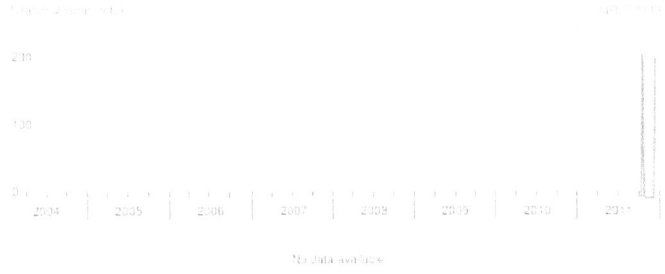

Figure 25: Performance Management Plan (accessed on the 9.2.2012)

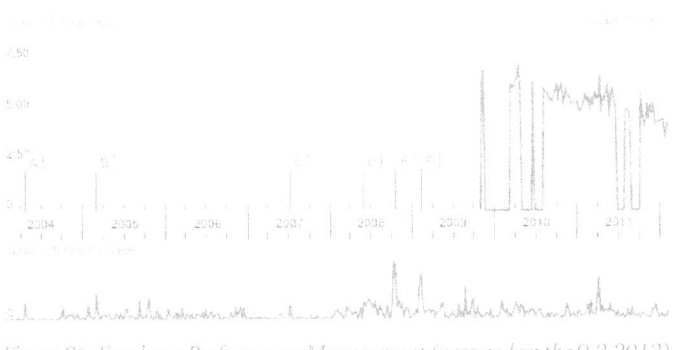

Figure 26: Employee Performance Management (accessed on the 9.2.2012)

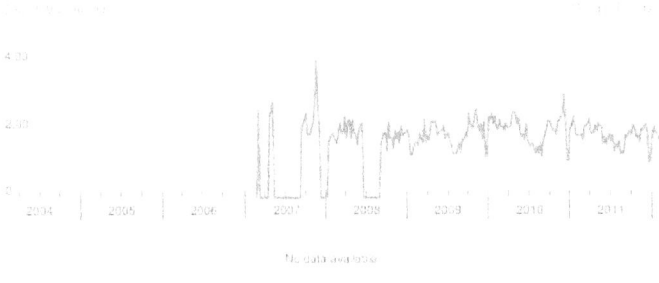

Figure 27: Personal Development Plan (accessed on the 9.2.2012)

"The Imperial Rater of Nine Grade seldom rates men according to their merits, but always according to his likes and dislikes"
Sin Yu

Access the most comprehensive and well documented selection of KPI examples

20,000 KPI examples
7,100 KPIs defined
2,700 KPIs documented in detail
15 Functional areas
24 Industries
3 Contexts

EXPLORER
$39
6 months access

Features

- ✓ Basic access
- ✓ Explore the complete catalogue
- ✓ Use advanced search
- ✓ View KPI definitions
- ✓ Save KPI examples

Numbers

- ✓ Browse 7000+ KPI examples
- ✓ Access 17 documentation fields
- ✓ View 200 documented KPIs

Research

One research report:
- ✓ Top 20 KPIs of 2010

Most Popular

PREMIUM
$249
12 months access

Features

- ✓ Explorer benefits plus
- ✓ Export of KPI examples in PDF format
- ✓ Edit the number of KPIs listed per page
- ✓ Filter by views, rating and documentation status
- ✓ Access to all documentation fields

Numbers

- ✓ Browse 7000+ KPI examples
- ✓ Access 17 documentation fields
- ✓ View 200 documented KPIs

Research

Two research reports:
- ✓ Top 20 KPIs of 2010
- ✓ Top 25 KPIs of 2010 report of your choice

INSIGHT
$999
12 months access

Features

- ✓ Premium benefits plus
- ✓ Online access to all research reports published in The KPI Institute's Insight Library
- ✓ There are over 25 reports published each year

Numbers

- ✓ Browse 7000+ KPI examples
- ✓ Access 40 documentation fields
- ✓ Export 1000 documented KPIs

Research

Three generic Excel templates pre-populated with over 70 KPI examples:
- ✓ Balanced Scorecard
- ✓ KPI Dashboard
- ✓ Performance Healthogram

Testimonials

On smartKPIs.com premium content

"Guys we are very thankful of the hard work you do. Your website really guides us on the daily performance management of our organization."

Omphile Macheng, Botswana

"Really a very good and useful website, I am excited about the content and comprehensiveness of data on your website, and I will recommend it to all professional in the governmental sector in United Arab of Emirates, Wish you all the best."

Mahdi El Horchi, United Arab Emirates

"Access to all smartKPIs.com research reports and advance functionality in searching the online catalogue helps my office in facilitating the understanding, selection and usage of KPIs across the organization."

Andrew Fraser, United Kingdom

On our publications

"The Top 25 Call Center KPIs of 2010 helps in understanding all the performance measures which should be taken into account to optimize performance..."

Jacob Brown, United States

"smartKPIs.com provided a simple yet powerful scorecard and dashboard model to start building our own with our business intelligence tools."

Humberto E Della Torre, El Salvador

"I was pleasantly surprised of the level of experience and knowledge of the smartKPIs.com team. The toolkit delivered was what I had anticipated to be."

Alex Giammona, Australia

*smart*KPIs.com

The *smart* choice in performance management

Media Exposure

Analysing the popularity of the discipline by evaluating media exposure.

Figures 28 and 29 were compiled according to data extracted from the archives of Google News as of 15 February 2012. As there was no significant number of search results prior to 2000, the starting year was set as the year 2000. The illustrations show the number of the search results on Google News for each keyword, between 2000 and 2011, logarithmically scaled against the corresponding years.

Figure 28 outlines that the media presence of the key terms can roughly be divided into five periods.

In the first period, the media exposure increased steeply from 2001 onwards, plateauing between 2003 and 2004. The second period, which was more stable, lasted until 2006. In the third period,

starting with 2007, the media exposure spiked. What is interesting to observe is the slump behaviors of the keywords during the Global Financial Crisis (2008 to 2010), partly because it only peaks negatively during 2010. Finally, there was a new trend coming up. The exposure after 2010 – in period 5 – exceeded the peak values of period 3 and gave the impression that there is a current upwards trend happening.

As the number of searches of each term increases, these trends become more stable. More interesting is the stable, overall increase of Strategic Management within the consciousness of the media.

Comparing 2010 with 2011, it is clear that most of the terms improved in media exposure. The terms "Performance

Management", "Business Management" and "Strategy Management" more than doubled in exposure. "Strategy Execution" was used nearly three times as often in 2011 than in 2010 and "Corporate Performance Management" experienced the biggest gain with an increase of more than three-rate exposure in period 5.

There is significant evidence that the first period describes the introduction of these managerial constructs into the wider professional community. After establishing a place in language and media, the terms plateaued and only increased in usage after years of mostly sustained global economic growth. This increase in attention found a sudden but to-be-expected downfall during the recession. In times where businesses

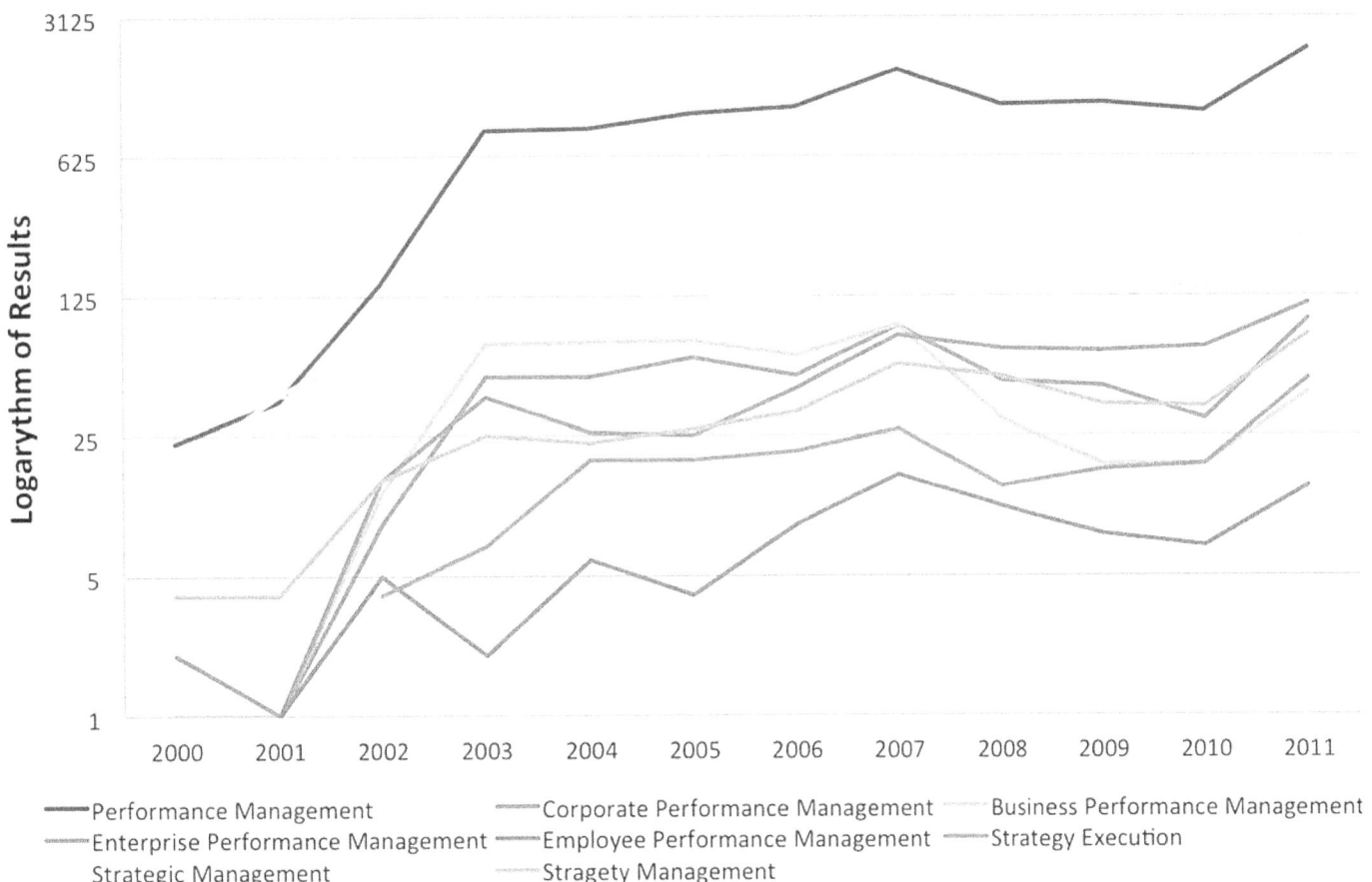

Figure 28: Level of Media Exposure in the Area of Performance Management

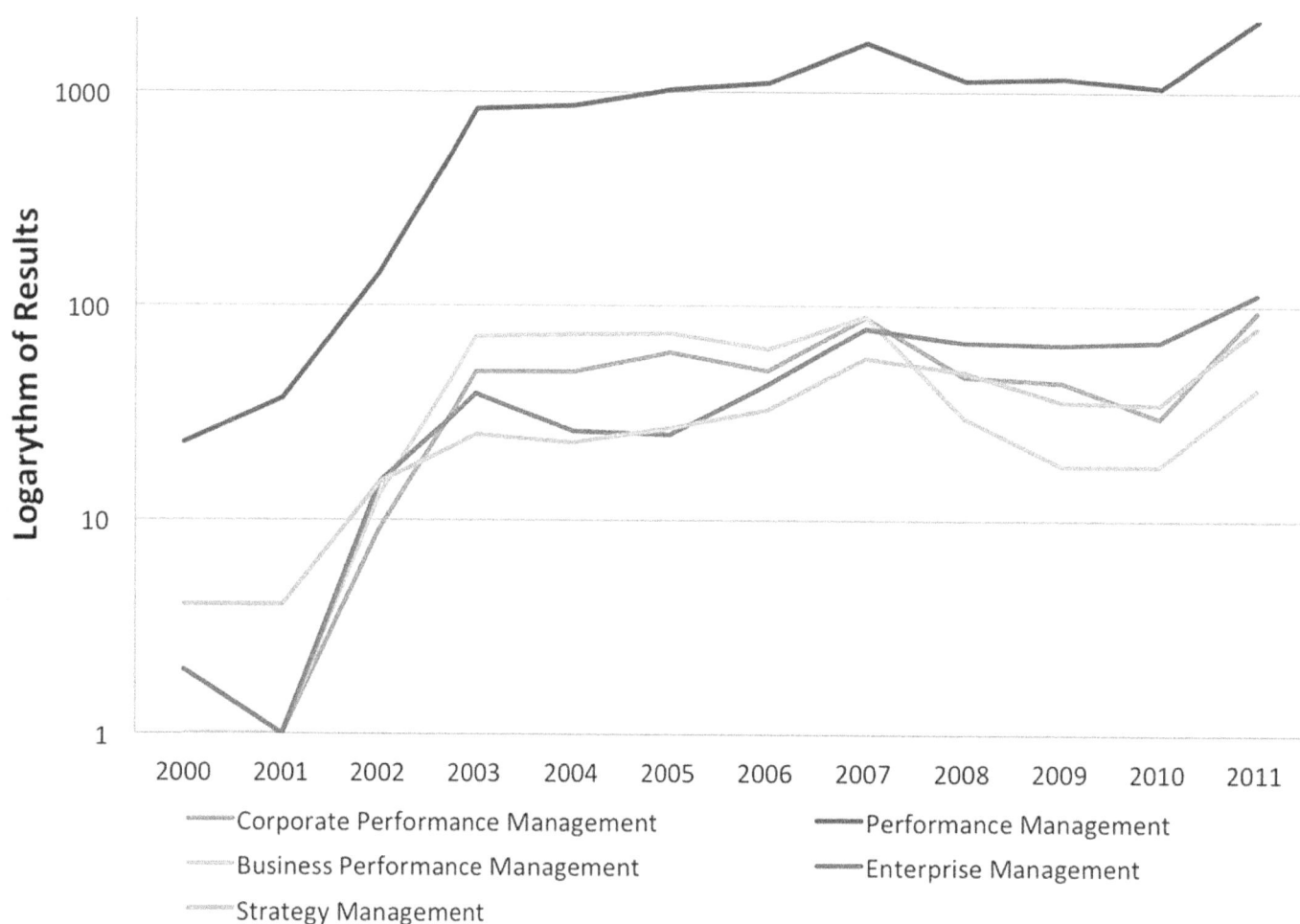

News trends of selected keywords

Logarythm of Results

Legend:
- Corporate Performance Management
- Business Performance Management
- Strategy Management
- Performance Management
- Enterprise Management

Figure 29: Level of Media Exposure for Performance Management keywords (cont.)

had to cut research and innovation expenses which led to a far more conservative view on Performance Management, media seemed to emphasise the financials more than the innovations. Still, the worst decrease in exposure lay by one third and occurred in period three.

This overall relatively stable behavior makes the current growth trend even more remarkable and it seems like a strong indicator that the media exposure will further increase over the next years. ▪

Performance Management Keywords:

Corporate Performance Management	Strategic Performance Management	Employee Performance Management
Business Performance Management	**Performance Management**	Strategy Execution
Enterprise Performance Management	Operational Performance Management	Strategy Management and Individual Performance Management

Educational Programs

The popularity of university degrees with a Performance Management focus seems to be on the rise. Over the last 15 years, many programs that had a component of Performance Management were launched around the world. These programs ranged from a Certificate to Bachelor, Master and MBA degrees.

One of the world's top business schools, Wharton Business School of the University of Pennsylvania (USA), has established Bachelor and MBA degrees specialising in Strategic Management. Another example is the Graduate Certificate in Performance Audit and Evaluation, offered by University of Canberra in Australia. However, it appears that Master level degrees with majors in Performance or Strategic Management are the more popular type of degrees.

Master degrees with Performance Management specializations are provided by a wide range of universities, including but not limited to: Cranfield University (Master in Managing Organizational Performance), Aarhus University (Master in Business Performance Management), Aston University (Master of Operational Research & Performance Management), University of Leicester (Master of Operational Research & Performance Management) and The University of Adelaide (Master of Commerce (Performance Management).

Table 4 provides more detailed and comprehensive information regarding the degrees which have a focus on Performance Management in 2012, at the international level. Apart from Performance Management degrees, a wide range of universities around the world offer subjects on Strategic or Performance Management as well. Both the degrees and subjects are ranked in alphabetical order, in accordance with the name of the institution. ▩

Table 4: Educational Institutions which offer degrees in Performance Management

University	Logo	Continent	Country	Degrees/Diploma	Duration	Related Topics/Subjects	Cost (2012 fees, per year)
Aarhus University Aarhus School of Business		Europe	Denmark	Master in Business Performance Management	2 years	- Strategy and Management (Danish) - Business Informatics (Danish) - Business Administration and Business Law (Danish) - Finance and International Business (English) - Business Performance Management (English)	EU citizens: Free Non-EU citizens: €9000
Aston University		Europe	UK	Master of Operational Research & Performance Management	1 year	- Effective Management Consultancy - Operational Research Methods - Data Mining for Managerial Decision Making - Advanced Performance Measurement Performance Management in Practice - Simulation for Managerial Decision Making - Advanced Spreadsheets & Databases	UK/EU: £10,500 International: £16000
Beihang University		Asia	China	Master of Business Intelligence and Enterprise Performance Management (part-time)	2.5 years	- Enterprise Information Strategy - Enterprise Risk and Internal Control - Operation Design and Supply Chain Management - Financial Performance Evaluation - Balanced Scorecard - Enterprise Indicators Modelling and Design	CNY ¥65,700
Cranfield University		Europe	UK	Executive (part-time) Master in Managing Organizational Performance	2 years	- Managing Organisational Performance - Strategic Performance - Decisions and Actions - Measuring Organisational Performance - Data Automation - Reward and Evaluation - Culture and Change Management - Performance Improvement - Reviewing Organisational Performance	£17,000
The University of Adelaide (Faculty of the Professions)		Australia	Australia	Master of Commerce (Performance Management)	1.5 years full-time	- Management Practice - Business Communications - Strategic Management I9 - Strategic Compensation Management - Knowledge Management & Measurement - Strategic Evaluation & Control	International Students: AUD $29,000
University of Canberra Faculty of Business and Government		Australia	Australia	Graduate Certificate in Performance Audit and Evaluation	1 year full-time 2 years part-time	- Performance Audit and Evaluation G1 - Performance Audit and Evaluation G2 - Human Resource Management - Management Ethics I15 - Organisational Behaviour F15 - Statistical Analysis & Decision Making	AUD $15,990 per year

University	Logo	Continent	Country	Degrees/ Diploma	Duration	Related Topics/Subjects	Cost (2012 fees, per year)
University of Leicester	University of Leicester	Europe	UK	Master in Performance Management and Workplace Learning (distance learning)	Flexible (Distance learning)	- Module 1 Employee Development and Workplace Learning - Module 2 The Organisation of Work and Organisational Performance - Module 3 Option Module - Module 4 Research Methods	£7335
University of Liege HEC Management School	Université de Liège	Europe	Belgium	Master in Business Management (Performance Management Systems)	2 years	- Business Game - Project Management - Change Management (English language) - Business Process Management - Enterprise Modelling and IT (English language) - Global Performance Management (English language) - Quality and Performance in operations Management (English language) - Advanced Management Control (English language)	- EU citizen: €1923 per year - Non-EU citizen: €1923 - €3845 (dependent on citizenship)
University of Pennsylvania Wharton Business School	Wharton	North America	USA	MBA of Strategic Management	2 years	- Competitive Strategy - Global Strategic Management - Strategy and Competitive Advantage - Organizational Economics and Strategy - Strategic Implementation - Multinational Business Strategy - Advanced Study Project in Strategic Management - Strategic Management of Human Assets - Managing Organizational Change - Information/Industry Structure and Competitive Strategy - Managerial Decision Making	USD $89,200 (includes tuition, fees and living expenses)
University of Pennsylvania Wharton Business School	Wharton	North America	USA	Bachelor of Management (Specialization in Strategic Management)	3-4 years	- Business Strategy and Policy - Competitive Strategy - Management of Technology - Organization Design - Corporate Governance - Strategic Implementation	USD $42,098 (includes tuition fees)

Educational Programs

Table 5: Performance Management University subjects

Country	University/School	Subjects	Related Degrees
		Europe	
UK	University of Cambridge	Strategic Performance Management	Professional Development Program
		Strategic Management: Creating and Sustaining Competitive Advantage	Professional Development Program
	University of Oxford	Managing Performance	Masters in Major Programme Management
	Heriot - Watt University Edinburgh Business School	Performance Management	MBA Master in Human Resource Management
	University of Bradford Bradford University School of Management	Understanding Strategic Management	Bachelor (Hons) Business Studies and Law
Netherlands	Maastricht School of Management	Measurement and Strategic Performance Management	EMBA Sustainability focus
		Strategic Management	EMBA Facility Management

Country	University/School	Subjects	Related Degrees
		North America	
USA	University of Pennsylvania Wharton Business School	Corporate Transactions & Strategy	Undergraduate Course
		Seminar in Corporate Strategy	Undergraduate Course
		Strategic Implementation	Undergraduate Course
	Boston College University Carroll School of Management	Strategy & Policy	Undergraduate Course
		Management & Operations	Undergraduate Course
		Operations, Strategy, & Consulting	Undergraduate Course
		Service Operations Management	Undergraduate Course
		Strategic Planning and Implementation	Undergraduate Course
Canada	University of Ottawa Telfer School of Management	Performance Management: Business Process Modeling	MBA
		Performance Management	MBA
		South America	
Peru	Centrum – Catolica	Strategic Management	International MBA
		Strategic Management and Leadership	DBA (Triple)
		Australia	
Australia	The University of Adelaide Business School	Strategic Management	MBA
	The University of Melbourne	Strategic Performance Management	Postgraduate Management Course
		Enterprise Performance Management	Undergraduate Course
		Asia	
Hong Kong	The Hong Kong University of Science and Technology	Strategic Management in China	Undergraduate Management Course
		Strategic Management	Postgraduate Management Course
		Strategic Management in China	Postgraduate Management Course
	The Chinese University of Hong Kong	Strategic Management	MBA
Singapore	National University of Singapore	Strategic Management	Bachelor of Business Administration (Accountancy)
	Nanyang Business School	Performance Management & HR Metrics	Undergraduate Course
		Performance Management and Appraisals	Professional Development Courses
		Strategic Talent Management & Performance Development	Professional Development Courses
		Africa	
South Africa	University of Cape Town Graduate School of Business	Strategy	MBA

Main Events

Introduction

Over the last two decades, the popularity of Performance Management events and conferences has been on the rise. There have been events targeted at both academics and practitioners.

In 2012, five major academic conferences will be hosted in Indonesia, Serbia, the Netherlands, UK and Czech Republic, while nine events targeted at practitioners are planned in the US, the UAE, Australia and Germany. Events in Performance Management specialization are spread throughout the year, from January to December and generally range from 2 to 6 days.

Due to the different natures of the events, such as purpose and target audience, fees for academic events tend to be lower than practitioner events, with an average fee of around US$300 and US$1000, respectively.

Table 6 provides more detailed and comprehensive information regarding the events in Performance Management in 2012. The information was correct at the time of research. ▣

Table 6: Performance Management events in 2012

Date	Logo	Title	Type	Location	Duration	Organiser	Fees
29-30 Jan		Corporate Performance Management Conference - Accelerating High Performance: Tactics, Tools, Technology	Practitioner	New York, US	2 Days	CFO Publishing LLC	$695 - $3295
27-29 Feb		8th HR Metrics & Performance Measurement Summit	Practitioner	Miami, US	2 Days	International Quality & Productivity Center (IQPC)	$549 - $2499
1-2 Mar		2012 Hampton Roads Business Management Conference	Practitioner	Virginia Beach, US	2 Days	Strategic Management Institute	$195 - $1175
6-8 Mar		Mission-Driven Management Summit 2012	Practitioner	Washington DC, US	3 Days	Ascendant Strategy Management Group	$795 - $1890
26-28 Mar		Strategic Performance Management & Measurement	Practitioner	Atlanta, US	3 Days	International Quality & Productivity Center (IQPC) The Balanced Scorecard Institute	$549 - $2899
21-26 Apr		Balanced Scorecard Forum 2012	Practitioner	Dubai, United Arab Emirates	6 Days	The Institute for International Research (IRR ME)	$995 - $5680
7 - 8 May		2nd Annual International Conference on Business Strategy and Organizational Behaviour BizStrategy 2012	Academic	Bali, Indonesia	2 Days	Global Science & Technology Forum (GSTF)	SGD 400 - 1250
15-16 May		Developing & Monitoring Key Performance Indicators in Government	Practitioner	Canberra, Australia	3 Days	Criterion Conferences Pty Ltd	AUD $3189 - $3519
5-9 Jun		SymOrg Symposium	Academic	Zlatibor, Serbia	5 Days	Innovative Management & Business Performance	€20 - €150
6-8 Jun		EURAM '12	Academic	Rotterdam, Netherlands	3 Days	Rotterdam School of Management (RSM), Erasmus University	€100 - €833
11-13 Jul		PMA 2012 Conference: From Strategy to Delivery	Academic	Cambridge, UK	3 Days	The Performance Management Association (PMA)	£195 - £395
18-19 Sep		Business Performance Forum 2012	Practitioner	Berlin, Germany	2 Days	World Trade Group (WTP)	GBP 1564 - 2081
7-9 Oct		SMS 32nd Annual International Conference	Academic	Prague, Czech Republic	3 Days	Strategic Management Society (SMS)	N/A
8 - 12 Dec		Balanced Scorecard Saudi Arabia 2012	Practitioner	Riyadh, Saudi Arabia	5 Days	The Institute for International Research (IRR ME)	$895 - $5185

Table 7: Past Performance Management events

Date	Year	Duration	Country	City	Title	Organiser
3-7 Dec	2011	5 Days	Saudi Arabia	Riyadh	Balanced Scorecard Saudi Arabia 2012	IRR ME
9-10 Nov	2011	2 Days	US	San Diego	Palladium 2011 Americas Summit	Palladium Group, Inc
6-9 Nov	2011	4 Days	US	Miami	SMS 31st Annual International Conference	Strategic Management Society (SMS)
18 Oct	2011	1 Day	US	San Francisco	Successful Strategy Execution Using Scorecards	Northern California Human Resources Association
11-13 Sep	2011	3 Days	US	Dallas	The 2011 CFO Corporate Performance Management Conference: Improving Business Analysis and Bottom-Line Performance	CFO Publishing LLC
25 Jun	2011	1 Day	India	Kolkata	1st International Conference on Business, Strategy & Management	Veloxian learning & Consultancy and American Hospitality Academy USA
7-9 Jun	2011	3 Days	UK	London	Palladium 2011 EMEA Summit	Palladium Group, Inc
1-4 Jun	2011	4 Days	Estonia	Tallinn	EURAM '11	Estonian Business School
26-31 Mar	2011	6 Days	United Arab Emirates	Dubai	Balanced Scorecard Forum 2011	IRR ME
8-10 Mar	2011	3 Days	US	Washington DC	Mission-Driven Management Summit 2011	GSMI & Ascendant Strategy Management Group
9-12 Jun	2010	4 Days	Serbia	Zlatibor	SymOrg Symposium 2010	University of Belgrade, Faculty of Organizational Sciences
24-26 Jun	2010	3 Days	Italy	Matera	International Forum on Knowledge Assets Dynamics	The Performance Management Association (PMA)
14-17 April	2009	3 Days	New Zealand	Dunedin	PMA 2009 Conference	The Performance Management Association (PMA)
26-27 Jun	2008	2 Days	Italy	Matera	International Forum on Knowledge Assets Dynamics	The Performance Management Association (PMA)
24-25 Jan	2008	2 Days	Switzerland	Lausanne	PMA Symposium/Long Range Planning Workshop	The Performance Management Association (PMA)
22-23 Jun	2007	2 Days	Italy	Matera	PMA supported event - International Forum on Knowledge Assets Dynamics	The Performance Management Association (PMA)

Job Trends

Career Prospects and Development

One key indicator used to illustrate the importance and growth rate of Performance Management is the number of available positions that relate to this concept. This study focused on six continents and two major job markets and used their most popular job websites to research the number of positions that were offered in these areas.

The following tables outline information on the job markets for roles such as Performance Manager, Strategy Manager and Performance Management: an estimate of available positions, as well as the proportion of positions available per continent and website.

Table 8: Performance Manager Jobs (13th of February 2012)

No.	Continent & Market	Job website	No. of jobs	Proportion
1	North America	www.monster.com	163	9.12%
2	Europe	www.jobsite.com.uk	19	1.06%
3	Asia	www.jobstreet.com	10	0.56%
4	Australia	www.seek.com.au	37	2.07%
5	China	www.zhaopin.com	474	26.51%
6	Africa	www.findajobinafrica.com	395	22.09%
7	South America	www.trabajos.com	31	1.73%
8	Middle East	www.bayt.com	659	36.86%
	Total		1788	100.00%

Table 9: Strategy Manager Jobs (13th of February 2012)

No.	Continent & Market	Job website	No. of jobs	Proportion
1	North America	www.monster.com	398	31.97%
2	Europe	www.jobsite.com.uk	19	1.53%
3	Asia	www.jobstreet.com	2	0.16%
4	Australia	www.seek.com.au	45	3.61%
5	China	www.zhaopin.com	47	3.78%
6	Africa	www.findajobinafrica.com	353	28.35%
7	South America	www.trabajos.com	28	2.25%
8	Middle East	www.bayt.com	353	28.35%
	Total		1245	100.00%

Table 10: Performance Management Jobs (13th of February 2012)

No.	Continent & Market	Job website	No. of jobs	Proportion
1	North America	www.monster.com	1015	6.38%
2	Europe	www.jobsite.com.uk	335	2.11%
3	Asia	www.jobstreet.com	193	1.21%
4	Australia	www.seek.com.au	1306	8.21%
5	China	www.zhaopin.com	11820	74.30%
6	Africa	www.findajobinafrica.com	503	3.16%
7	South America	www.trabajos.com	78	0.49%
8	Middle East	www.bayt.com	659	4.14%
	Total		15909	100.00%

Note: the results in China are the sum of both English and Chinese keywords searches, which may contain double counted positions, however, due to the language barrier, the portion could be small.

In absolute terms, it is clear that the total count on job positions related to "Performance Management" is higher than those on "Performance Manager" and "Strategy Manager". This indicates that the demand for "Performance Management" knowledge and skills is vast and by no means limited to specific job profiles.

In relative terms, the charts make clear that the number of jobs in China, Africa and Middle East is higher than on other continents. This may be due to the increasing demand for skills and knowledge related to Performance Management in 2012.

Overall, this gives us a clear picture of the skills on the job markets of China, Africa and the Middle East, hence away from the western parts of the world. Although the duration of this trend can not be measured through this particular way of reasoning, taking into account economic growth and the long binding nature of such proficiency, it seems only reasonable to assume that this is a steady trend. ■

THE KPI INSTITUTE   PERFORMANCE MANAGEMENT EDUCATION

OPEN COURSES OF 1-3 DAYS

- PARTICIPANTS FROM OVER 20 COUNTRIES ATTENDED OUR PROGRAMS OVER THE LAST 12 MONTHS
- ORGANIZED IN AUSTRALIA, INDONESIA, MALAYSIA, ROMANIA, SOUTH AFRICA, SAUDI ARABIA, THAILAND, TURKEY, UAE, UK AND USA

IN-HOUSE PROGRAMS OF 2-4 DAYS

- CUSTOMIZED TO CLIENT NEEDS
- DELIVERED AT CLIENT PREMISES

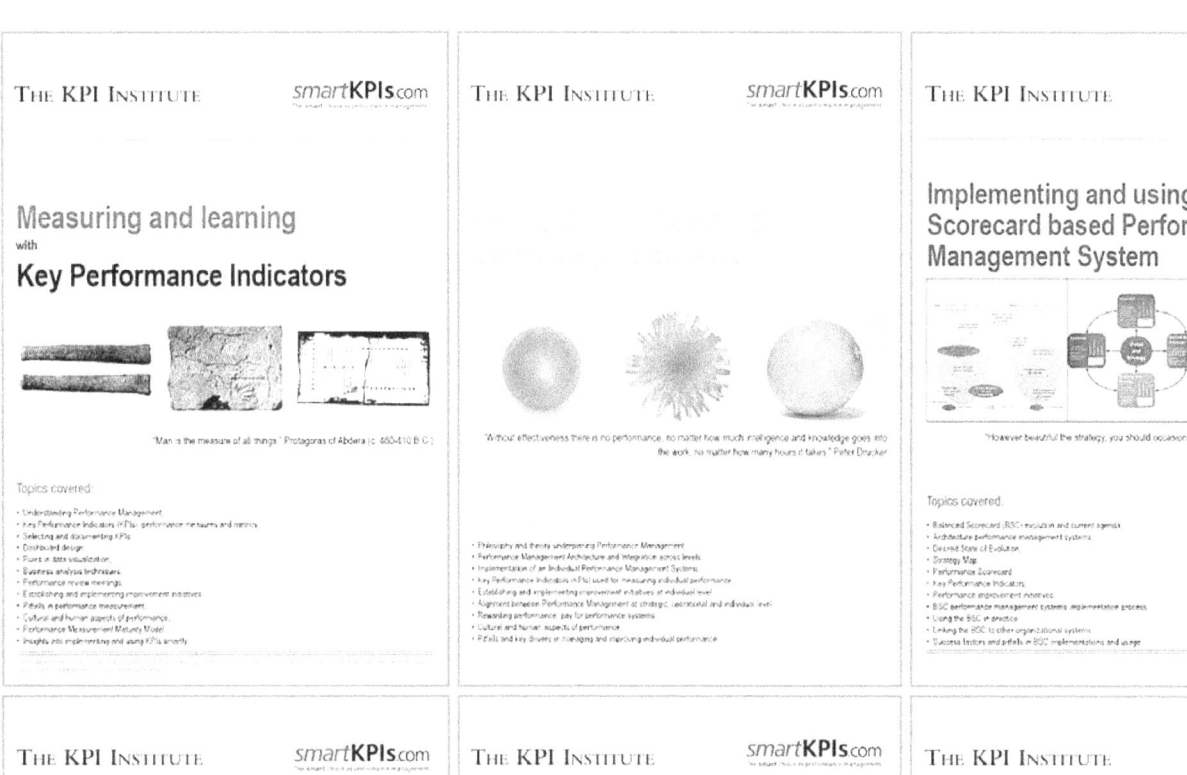

www.smartkpis.com/premium/services/training/browse-performance-management-courses

Salaries

The following two tables show salary ranges for Performance Managers and Strategy Managers, as well as the range differences in various industries ranked after average salary.

The highest and the lowest salaries are based on the open positions found on the job websites listed before. One has to acknowledge that this may reflect salaries and demand from, mostly, western markets. The salary ranges are estimated and therefore the accuracy may be affected. In addition, Senior Performance Managers roles included in this list will have a higher salary than the average. Hence, industries which are looking for proportionally more Senior Performance Managers (e.g. Business Services) will have a higher salary average.

Industry information could not be obtained for all industries, therefore the salary ranges could not be estimated. ▪

Table 11: Performance Manager Salary Ranges

Performance Manager

Highest	$258K
Lowest	$25K

Industries	Range
Financial Services	$85k - $258k
Business Services	$73k - $256k
Energy & Utilities	$80k - $131k
Beverages	$100k - $109k
Insurance	$73k - $126k
Construction	$92k - $99k
Computer Software	$46k - $152k
Consumer Products Manufacturers	$73k - $99k
Computer Services	$80k - $87k
Government	$73k - $91k
Electronics	$76k - $84k
Health Care	$48k - $99k
Consumer Services	$47k - $82k
Education	$27k - $38k
Industries With No Data Available	**Ranked after average**
Aerospace & Defence	
Agriculture	
Automotive & Transport	
Banking	
Charitable Organizations	
Chemicals	
Computer Hardware	
Cultural Institutions	
Environmental Services & Equipment	
Food	
Foundations	
Industrial Manufacturing	
Leisure	
Media	
Membership Organizations	

Table 12: Strategy Manager Salary Ranges

Strategy Manager

Highest	$245K
Lowest	$34K

Industries	Range
Financial Services	$124k - $245k
Business Services	$124k - $245k
Environmental Services & Equipment	$144k - $157k
Energy & Utilities	$97k - $198k
Banking	$79k - $209k
Construction	$139k - $149k
Beverage	$110k - $157k
Computer Hardware	$62k - $200k
Computer Services	$62k - $200k
Food	$118k - $131k
Computer Software	$85k - $150k
Health Care	$85k - $143k
Media	$75k - $136k
Consumer Products Manufacturers	$87k - $115k
Electronics	$87k - $113k
Insurance	$87k - $113k
Industrial Manufacturing	$87k - $112k
Consumer Services	$89k - $102k
Automotive & Transport	$58k - $125k
Education	$82k - $89k
Leisure	$58k - $106k
Chemicals	$67k - $72k
Charitable Organizations	$60k - $65k
Industries With No Data Available	**Ranked after average**
Aerospace & Defence	
Agriculture	
Cultural Institutions	
Foundations	
Government	
Membership Organizations	

Bestselling Books

Performance Management has a fair share of Bestselling books, in various areas of interest. For identifying them, ten keywords were selected based on their relevance to Performance Management.

Results were generated using Amazon.com. Their relevance the list reflects manually verified results as the tags of "performance" by Amazon are understandably very broad. Despite this, Amazon was the best available source of information, given the size of its database and reputation. Furthermore, the rankings were based on the date when the research was launched; therefore, changes may have occurred since.

The Top 10 books are listed below. ▪

Table 13: Top 10 Books on "Performance Management" (8th of February 2012)

Performance Management

No.	Title	Author	Published
1	The Power of Full Engagement: Managing Energy, Not Time, Is the Key to High Performance and Personal Renewal	Jim Loehr & Tony Schwartz	2004
2	The Advantage: Why Organizational Health Trumps Everything Else In Business	Patrick Lencioni	2012
3	Uncommon Service: How to Win by Putting Customers at the Core of Your Business	Frances Frei & Anne Morriss	2012
4	The Four Obsessions of an Extraordinary Executive: A Leadership Fable	Patrick Lencioni	2000
5	Topgrading: How Leading Companies Win by Hiring, Coaching, and Keeping the Best People, Revised and Updated Edition	Bradford D. Smart Ph.D.	2005
6	Leading at a Higher Level, Revised and Expanded Edition: Blanchard on Leadership and Creating High Performing Organizations	Ken Blanchard	2009
7	Balanced Scorecards and Operational Dashboards with Microsoft Excel	Ron Person	2008
8	Engine Management: Advanced Tuning	Greg Banish	2007
9	HR Transformation: Building Human Resources From the Outside In	Dave Ulrich et al	2009
10	Beyond Performance Management: Why, When, and How to Use 40 Tools and Best Practices for Superior Business Performance	Jeremy Hope et al	2012

Corporate Performance Management

No.	Title	Author	Published
1	Profiles in Performance: Business Intelligence Journeys and the Roadmap for Change	Howard Dresner	2009
2	Five Key Principles of Corporate Performance Management	Bob Paladino	2007
3	Innovative Corporate Performance Management: Five Key Principles to Accelerate Results	Bob Paladino	2010
4	Beyond Governance: Creating Corporate Value through Performance, Conformance and Responsibility	Martin Fahy et al	2005
5	Corporate Performance Management: How to build a better organization through measurement-driven, strategic alignment (Improving Human Performance)	David Wade et al	2001
6	Effective Strategy Execution: Improving Performance with Business Intelligence (Management for Professionals)	Bernd Heesen	2012
7	Handbook of Corporate Performance Management	Mike Bourne et al	2011
8	The Strategy Gap: Leveraging Technology to Execute Winning Strategies	Michael Coveney et al	2003
9	Corporate Performance Management: ARIS in Practice	August-Wilhelm Scheer et al	2006
10	Competitive Financial Operations, CFO book	www.CFOProject.com	2003

Business Performance Management

No.	Title	Author	Published
1	Time-Driven Activity-Based Costing: A Simpler and More Powerful Path to Higher Profits	Robert S. Kaplan et al	2007
2	Best Practices in Planning and Performance Management: From Data to Decisions (Wiley Best Practices)	David A. J. Axson	2007
3	The MAXIMO Manager's Guide to Business Performance Management	Richard Taggs et al	2011
4	The Business of Influence: Reframing Marketing and PR for the Digital Age	Philip Sheldrake	2011
5	The Performance Management Revolution: Business Results Through Insight and Action	Howard Dresner	2007
6	Dashboards: High-impact Strategies - What You Need to Know: Definitions, Adoptions, Impact, Benefits, Maturity, Vendors	Kevin Roebuck	2011
7	Microsoft PerformancePoint 2007 For Dummies	Rachel Blum et al	2008
8	Back to Business Basics	Dr Eileen Doyle	2010
9	Enterprise Management with SAP SEM(TM)/ Business Analytics (SAP Excellence)	Marco Meier et al	2005
10	Application Performance Management (APM): High-impact Strategies - What You Need to Know: Definitions, Adoptions, Impact, Benefits, Maturity, Vendors	Kevin Roebuck	2011

Table 16: Top 10 Books on "Enterprise Performance Management" (8th of February 2012)

Enterprise Performance Management

No.	Title	Author	Published
1	Oracle Hyperion Financial Management Tips And Techniques: Design, Implementation & Support (Oracle Press)	Peter John Fugere	2011
2	Look Smarter Than You Are with Hyperion Planning: An Administrator's Guide	Edward Roske et al	2010
3	Getting Started with Oracle Hyperion Planning 11	Reddy EntiSandeep	2011
4	Oracle Essbase& Oracle OLAP: The Guide to Oracle's Multidimensional Solution (Oracle Press)	Michael Schrader et al	2009
5	Planning and Implementing IT Portfolio Management: Maximizing the Return on Information Technology Investments	Edmund W. Fitzpatrick	2005
6	Enterprise Dashboards: Design and Best Practices for IT	Shadan Malik	2005
7	Look Smarter Than You Are with Oracle Hyperion Planning: An End User's Guide	Edward Roske et al	2010
8	Service Oriented Enterprises	Setrag Khoshafian	2006
9	CFO Insights: Delivering High Performance	Michael R. Sutcliff et al	2006
10	CFO Insights: Enabling High Performance Through Leading Practices for Finance ERP	C. CristianWulf	2006

Table 17: Top 10 Books on "Strategic Performance Management" (8th of February 2012)

Strategic Performance Management

No.	Title	Author	Published
1	Strengths-Based Leadership	Tom Rathet al	2009
2	Execution: The Discipline of Getting Things Done	Larry Bossidy et al	2002
3	How to Change the World: Social Entrepreneurs and the Power of New Ideas, Updated Edition	David Bornstein	2007
4	Competitive Strategy: Techniques for Analysing Industries and Competitors	Michael E. Porter	1998
5	Organizational Behavior: Improving Performance and Commitment in the Workplace	Jason Colquittet al	2010
6	Competitive Advantage: Creating and Sustaining Superior Performance	Michael E. Porter	1998
7	Competing on Analytics: The New Science of Winning	Thomas H. Davenport et al	2007
8	Data-Driven Marketing: The 15 Metrics Everyone in Marketing Should Know	Mark Jeffery	2010
9	The Other Side of Innovation: Solving the Execution Challenge (Harvard Business Review)	Vijay Govindarajanet al	2010
10	The Balanced Scorecard: Translating Strategy into Action	Robert S. Kaplan et al	1996

Operational Performance Manage

No.	Title	Author	Published
1	Balanced Scorecards and Operational Dashboards with Microsoft Excel	Ron Person	2008
2	Beyond Performance: How Great Organizations Build Ultimate Competitive Advantage	Scott Keller et al	2011
3	The Toyota Way to Continuous Improvement: Linking Strategy and Operational Excellence to Achieve Superior Performance	Jeffrey Liker et al	2011
4	The Strategy-Focused Organization: How Balanced Scorecard Companies Thrive in the New Business Environment	Robert S. Kaplan et al	2000
5	The Execution Premium: Linking Strategy to Operations for Competitive Advantage	Robert S. Kaplan et al	2008
6	Human Resource Champions	David Ulrich	1996
7	Measuring ITIL: Measuring, Reporting and Modelling - the IT Service Management Metrics That Matter Most to IT Senior Executives	Randy A. Steinberg	2001
8	The Human Equation: Building Profits by Putting People First	Jeffery Pfeffer	1998
9	Quality & Performance Excellence	James R. Evans	2010
10	Business Dashboards: A Visual Catalog for Design and Deployment	Nils H. Rasmussen et al	2009

Individual Performance Management

No.	Title	Author	Published
1	The Presentation of Self in Everyday Life	Erving Goffman	1959
2	The Progress Principle: Using Small Wins to Ignite Joy, Engagement, and Creativity at Work	Teresa Amabileet al	2011
3	Who's in the Room: How Great Leaders Structure and Manage the Teams Around Them	Bob Frisch	2012
4	The Wisdom of Teams: Creating the High-Performance Organization (Collins Business Essentials)	Jon R. Katzenbachet al	2003
5	Beyond Performance: How Great Organizations Build Ultimate Competitive Advantage (CourseSmart)	Scott Keller et al	2011
6	The New HR Analytics: Predicting the Economic Value of Your Company's Human Capital Investments	Jac Fitz-enz	2010
7	Creating Public Value: Strategic Management in Government	Mark Harrison Moore	1997
8	Human Resource Champions	David Ulrich	1996
9	The ROI of Human Capital: Measuring the Economic Value of Employee Performance	Jac Fitz-enz	2009
10	Becoming a Manager: How New Managers Master the Challenges of Leadership	Linda A. Hill	2003

Employee Performance Management

No.	Title	Author	Published
1	Strengths Finder 2.0	Tom Rath	2007
2	Strengths-Based Leadership	Tom Rathet al	2009
3	Psychology in Action, (Chapters 1-16)	Karen Huffman	2008
4	2600 Phrases for Effective Performance Reviews: Ready-to-Use Words and Phrases That Really Get Results	Paul Falcone	2005
5	Human Resource Management (Available Titles Coursemate)	Robert L. Mathis et al	2010
6	Conversations for Creating Star Performers: Go Beyond the Performance Review to Inspire Excellence Every Day	Shawn Kent Hayashi	2011
7	Uncommon Service: How to Win by Putting Customers at the Core of Your Business	Frances Freiet al	2012
8	101 Tough Conversations to Have with Employees: A Manager's Guide to Addressing Performance, Conduct, and Discipline Challenges	Paul Falcone	2009
9	Peak: How Great Companies Get Their Mojo from Maslow	Chip Conley et al	2007
10	Coaching for Performance: GROWing Human Potential and Purpose - The Principles and Practice of Coaching and Leadership, 4th Edition	Sir John Whitmore	2009

Strategy Execution

No.	Name	Author	Published
1	Deep Dive: The Proven Method for Building Strategy, Focusing Your Resources, and Taking Smart Action	Rich Horwath	2009
2	The Execution Premium: Linking Strategy to Operations for Competitive Advantage	Robert S. Kaplan et al	2008
3	Making Strategy Work: Leading Effective Execution and Change	Lawrence G. Hrebiniak	2005
4	Human Resource Champions	David Ulrich	1996
5	Building High Performance Government Through Lean Six Sigma: A Leader's Guide to Creating Speed, Agility, and Efficiency	Mark Price et al	2011
6	The Workforce Scorecard: Managing Human Capital To Execute Strategy	Mark A. Huselid et al	2005
7	Management Accounting: Information for Decision-Making and Strategy Execution (6th Edition)	Anthony A. Atkinson et al	2011
8	The Delta Model: Reinventing Your Business Strategy	Arnoldo C. Hax	2009
9	The Differentiated Workforce: Transforming Talent into Strategic Impact	Brian E. Becker et al	2009
10	Performance Management: Integrating Strategy Execution, Methodologies, Risk, and Analytics (Wiley and SAS Business Series)	Gary Cokins	2009

Table 22: Top 10 Books on "Strategic Management" (8th of February 2012)

Strategic Management

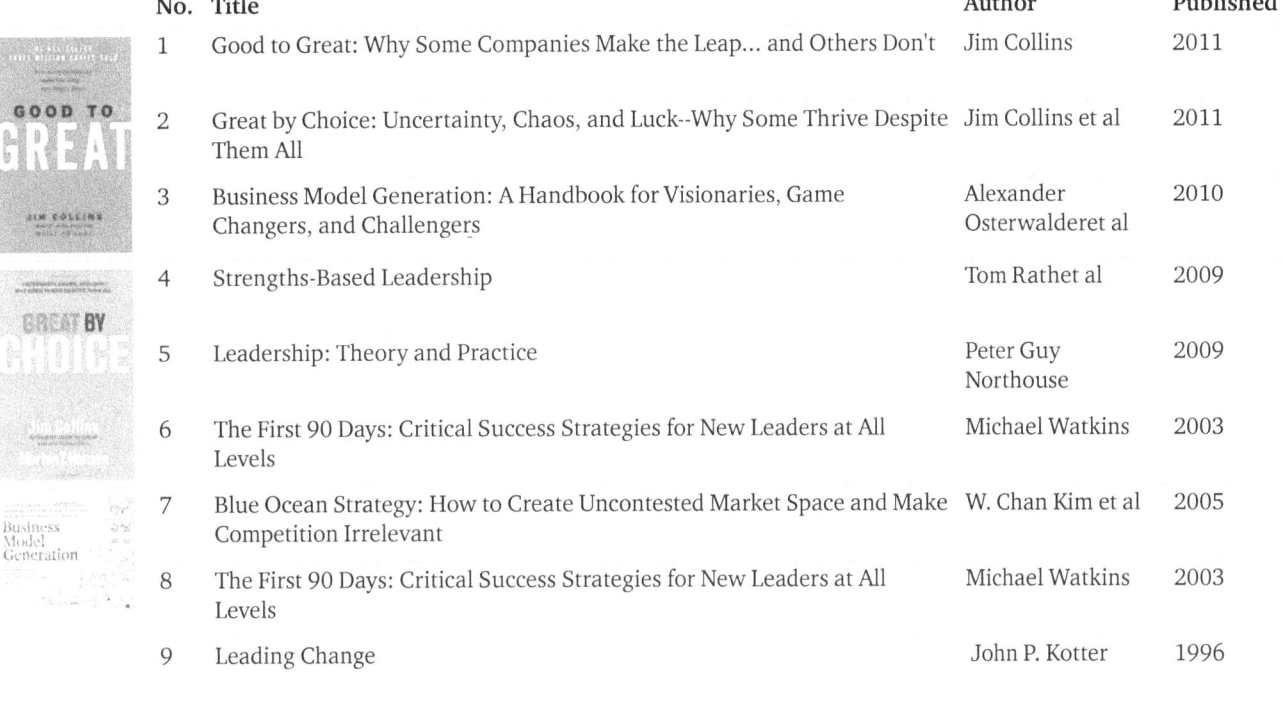

No.	Title	Author	Published
1	Good to Great: Why Some Companies Make the Leap... and Others Don't	Jim Collins	2011
2	Great by Choice: Uncertainty, Chaos, and Luck--Why Some Thrive Despite Them All	Jim Collins et al	2011
3	Business Model Generation: A Handbook for Visionaries, Game Changers, and Challengers	Alexander Osterwalderet al	2010
4	Strengths-Based Leadership	Tom Rathet al	2009
5	Leadership: Theory and Practice	Peter Guy Northouse	2009
6	The First 90 Days: Critical Success Strategies for New Leaders at All Levels	Michael Watkins	2003
7	Blue Ocean Strategy: How to Create Uncontested Market Space and Make Competition Irrelevant	W. Chan Kim et al	2005
8	The First 90 Days: Critical Success Strategies for New Leaders at All Levels	Michael Watkins	2003
9	Leading Change	John P. Kotter	1996
10	The Lean Six Sigma Pocket Toolbook: A Quick Reference Guide to 100 Tools for Improving Quality and Speed	Michael L. George et al	2004

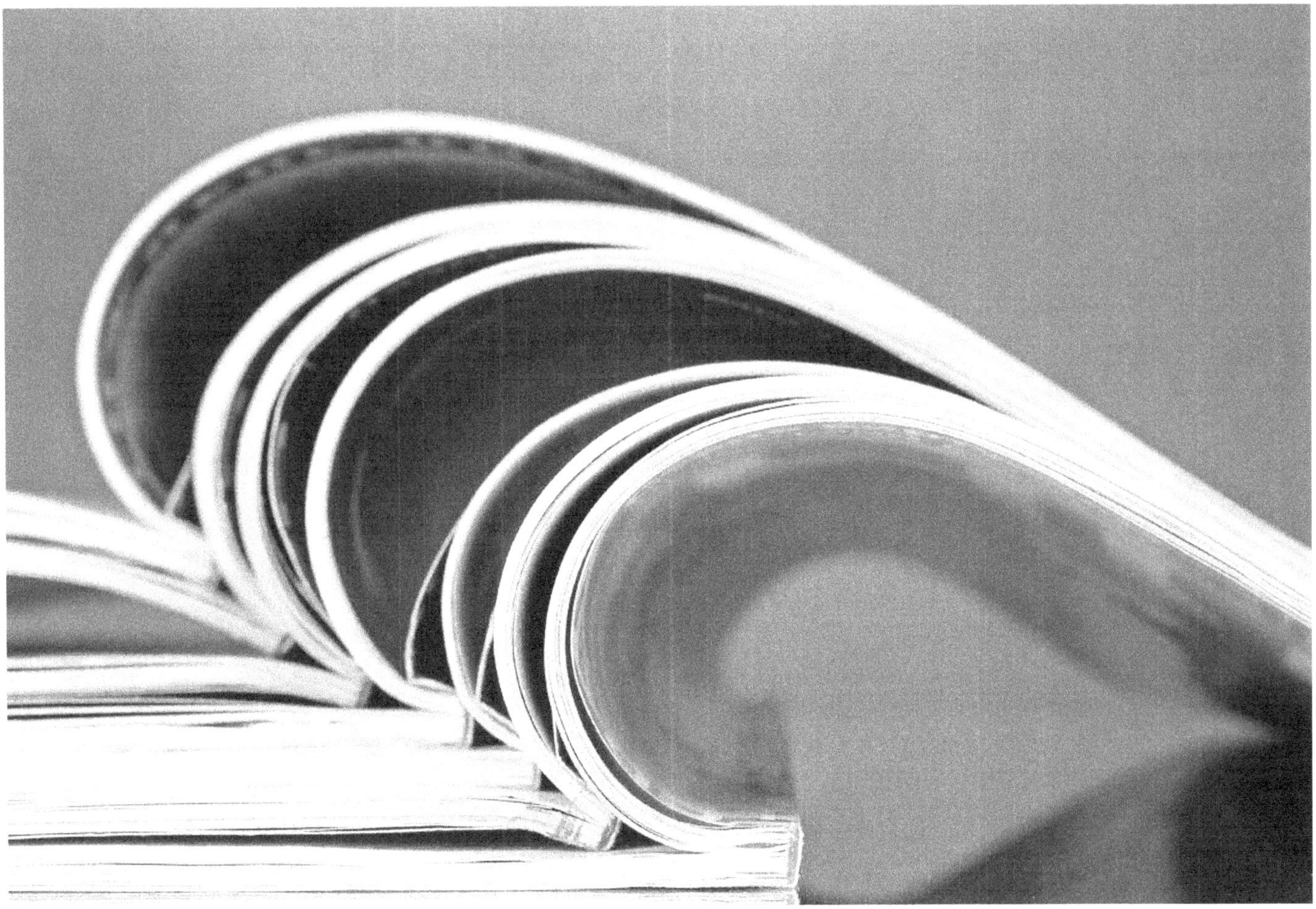

Latest Published Books

The lists of latest published books at the time of research (8th of February 2012) are ranked in the same manner as the list of Bestselling Books. It reflects an up-to-date overview about the focus and trends in Performance Management publishing. ▪

Table 23: The latest published books on "Performance Management" (8th of February 2012)

Performance Management

No.	Title	Author	Published
1	Beyond Performance Management: Why, When, and How to Use 40 Tools and Best Practices for Superior Business Performance	Jeremy Hope et al	2/7/2012
2	Uncommon Service: How to Win by Putting Customers at the Core of Your Business	Frances Freiet al	2/7/2012
3	The Crime Numbers Game: Management by Manipulation (Advances in Police Theory and Practice)	John A. Eternoet al	1/31/2012
4	Best Practice in Team Excellence: Using the International Team Excellence Award Framework to Improve Your Organization s Results	Laurie A. Broedlinget al	1/27/2012
5	How to Performance Benchmark Your Risk Management: A practical guide to help you tell if your risk management is effective	Mr Julian Talbot et al	1/26/2012
6	The Big Book of HR	Barbara Mitchell et al	1/22/2012
7	Performance Management (3rd Edition)	Herman Aguinis	1/20/2012
8	Lean but Agile: Rethink Workforce Planning and Gain a True Competitive Edge	William J. Rothwell et al	1/18/2012
9	Best Practices in Management Accounting	Greg N. Gregoriouet al	1/17/2012
10	Supporting and Supervising Mid-Level Professionals: New Directions for Student Services (J-B SS Single Issue Student Services)	Larry D. Roper	1/11/2012

Table 24: The latest published books on "Corporate Performance Management" (8th of February 2012)

Corporate Performance Management

No.	Title	Author	Published
1	Effective Strategy Execution: Improving Performance with Business Intelligence (Management for Professionals)	Bernd Heesen	1/3/2012
2	Handbook of Corporate Performance Management	Mike Bourne et al	11/29/2011
3	CPM Suites - Corporate Performance Management: High-impact Strategies - What You Need to Know: Definitions, Adoptions, Impact, Benefits, Maturity, Vendors	Kevin Roebuck	9/5/2011
4	Operational Business Intelligence (German Edition)	Christian Schmitz	2/16/2011
5	Corporate Performance Management: ARIS in Practice	August-Wilhelm Scheer et al	11/23/2010
6	Innovative Corporate Performance Management: Five Key Principles to Accelerate Results	Bob Paladino	11/9/2010
7	Profiles in Performance: Business Intelligence Journeys and the Roadmap for Change	Howard Dresner	11/9/2009
8	RT: Vol. 1: Chapter 8: The CEO's Triple Dilemma of Compensation, Employee, and Corporate Performance Management (The Refractive Thinker)	Dr. Lucy Surhyel Newman	4/1/2009
9	Corporate Performance Management mit SAP	ChristophHaldi	2008
10	Corporate Performance Management	Alexander Nyiri	10/31/2007

Business Performance Management

No.	Title	Author	Published
1	Business Performance Management for Telecommunications Operators: Customer and Service Assurance Perspective	Michael Orzessek et al	12/30/2011
2	CPM Suites - Corporate Performance Management: High-impact Strategies - What You Need to Know: Definitions, Adoptions, Impact, Benefits, Maturity, Vendors	Kevin Roebuck	9/5/2011
3	Dashboards: High-impact Strategies - What You Need to Know: Definitions, Adoptions, Impact, Benefits, Maturity, Vendors	Kevin Roebuck	9/2/2011
4	Performance Management, including: Business Performance Management, Meta Learning, Application Performance Management, Hyperion Planning, Performance ... Integrated Business Planning, Accelops	Hephaestus Books	9/1/2011
5	The MAXIMO Manager's Guide to Business Performance Management	Richard Taggs et al	1/3/2011
6	Back to Business Basics	Dr Eileen Doyle	9/7/2010
7	Business Performance Management Systems Proc. allowance - ("higher education") (neck)	Danko	2010
8	Business Performance Management Systems Proc. guide - (Textbooks for the program MBA ") (neck)	Abdikeev N.M.	2010
9	Does vertical integration affect firm performance? Evidence from the airline industry.: An article from: The Rand Journal of Economics (Blackwell)	Silke J. Forbes et al	11/29/2010
10	Procurement management using option contracts: random spot price and the portfolio effect.(Report): An article from: IIE Transactions	Qi Fu et al	4/13/2011

Enterprise Performance Management

No.	Title	Author	Published
1	Getting Started with Oracle Hyperion Planning 11	Reddy EntiSandeep	9/23/2011
2	Oracle Hyperion Financial Management Tips And Techniques: Design, Implementation & Support (Oracle Press)	Peter John Fugere	9/16/2011
3	Formation of the mechanism of enterprise Performance Management: a case of the food industry of Ukraine	Anatoliy Goncharuk	4/17/2011
4	Look Smarter Than You Are with Oracle Hyperion Planning: An End User's Guide	Edward Roskeet al	12/4/2010
5	Understanding SAP BusinessObjects Enterprise Performance Management	William D. Newman	7/30/2010
6	Look Smarter Than You Are with Hyperion Planning: An Administrator's Guide	Edward Roskeet al	7/12/2010
7	Oracle Essbase& Oracle OLAP: The Guide to Oracle's Multidimensional Solution (Oracle Press)	Michael Schrader et al	10/7/2009
8	Enterprise Performance Management: Concepts, Methods and Applications	CAI JIAN DENG	5/1/2007
9	Service Oriented Enterprises	SetragKhoshafian	10/9/2006
10	Enterprise Performance Management mit SAP	Michael Staade	4/30/2005

Table 27: The latest published books on "Strategic Performance Management" (8th of February 2012)

Strategic Performance Management

No.	Title	Author	Published
1	Corporate Social Responsibility and Business Performance: Theories and Evidence about Organizational Responsibility	Tobias Gössling	1/30/2012
2	The Practice of Enterprise Modeling: 4th IFIP WG 8.1 Working Conference, PoEM 2011 Oslo, Norway, November 2-3, 2011 Proceedings (Lecture Notes in Business Information Processing)	Paul Johannesson et al	1/26/2012
3	Organizational Behavior: Improving Performance and Commitment in the Workplace	Jason Colquitt et al	1/21/2012
4	Strategic Management: The Challenge of Creating Value	Peter FitzRoy et al	1/14/2012
5	The Oxford Handbook of Business and the Natural Environment (Oxford Handbooks)	PratimaBansal et al	1/13/2012
6	Effective Dashboard Design: Design Secrets to Getting More Value From Performance Dashboards	Gail La Grouw	1/5/2012
7	New Corporate Governance: Successful Board Management Tools	Martin Hilb	1/4/2012
8	Performance Measurement with the Balanced Scorecard: A Practical Approach to Implementation within SMEs (SpringerBriefs in Business)	Stefano Biazzo et al	1/4/2012
9	Effective Strategy Execution: Improving Performance with Business Intelligence (Management for Professionals)	Bernd Heesen	1/3/2012
10	Strategic Management and Public Service Performance	Rhys Andrews, George Boyne, Jennifer Law and Richard Walke	1/3/2012

Table 28: The latest published books on "Operational Performance Management" (8th of February 2012)

Operational Performance Management

No.	Title	Author	Published
1	Operational Mid-Level Management for Police	John L. Coleman	1/23/2012
2	Managing Performance in Turbulent Times: Analytics and Insight	Ed Barrows et al	12/6/2011
3	A How To Guide To Successfully Implementing a Quality Operational Excellence System	The Ninja Report TNR	11/18/2011
4	Public Management Reform: A Comparative Analysis - New Public Management, Governance, and the Neo-Weberian State	Christopher Pollitt et al	11/7/2011
5	Top 25 Business Consulting KPIs of 2010	smartKPIs.com et al	11/1/2011
6	Top 25 Call Center KPIs of 2010	smartKPIs.com et al	11/1/2011
7	Top 25 Customer Service KPIs of 2010	smartKPIs.com et al	11/1/2011
8	Top 25 Finance KPIs of 2010	smartKPIs.com et al	11/1/2011
9	Top 25 Healthcare KPIs of 2010	smartKPIs.com et al	11/1/2011
10	Top 25 Hotel KPIs of 2010	smartKPIs.com et al	11/1/2011

Table 29: The latest published books on "Individual Performance Management" (8th of February 2012)

Individual Performance Management

No.	Title	Author	Published
1	Who's in the Room: How Great Leaders Structure and Manage the Teams Around Them	Bob Frisch	1/24/2012
2	Relational Accountability: Complexities of Structural Injustice	Joy Moncrieffe	11/8/2011
3	Business Fundamentals	Donald J McCubbrey	12/14/2011
4	Managing Performance in Turbulent Times: Analytics and Insight	Ed Barrows et al	12/6/2011
5	Handbook of Corporate Performance Management	Mike Bourne et al	11/29/2011
6	Industrial Research Performance Management: Key Performance Indicators in the ICT Industry (Contributions to Management Science)	TatjanaSamsonowa	11/18/2011
7	Public Management Reform: A Comparative Analysis - New Public Management, Governance, and the Neo-Weberian State	Christopher Pollitt et al	11/7/2011
8	Assessment Centres and Global Talent Management	Nigel Povah et al	11/1/2011
9	Top 25 HR KPIs of 2010	smartKPIs.com et al	11/1/2011
10	Whatever Happened to Frank and Fearless?: The impact of new public management on the Australian Public Service	Kathy MacDermott	10/13/2011

Table 30: The latest published books on "Employee Performance Management" (8th of February 2012)

Employee Performance Management

No.	Title	Author	Published
1	Uncommon Service: How to Win by Putting Customers at the Core of Your Business	Frances Frei et al	2/7/2012
2	Managing Employee Performance: (case studies in both developed and developing countries)	Aun Falestien Faletehan et al	2/1/2012
3	Performance improvement through business processes: Developing and testing a model of employee and organizational performance through business processes	Arshad Zaheer et al	1/31/2012
4	Performance Management (3rd Edition)	Herman Aguinis	1/20/2012
5	Employee Engagement 2.0: How to Motivate Your Team for High Performance (A Real-World Guide for Busy Managers)	Kevin Kruse	1/23/2012
6	5 Easy Steps to Perfect Employee Performance	Sigrid de Kaste et al	1/12/2012
7	A Guide to Assessing Needs: Essential Tools for Collecting Information, Making Decisions, and Achieving Development Results	Ryan Watkins et al	1/6/2012
8	How to Improve Team Member Accountability (Team Building Tool Box for Busy Managers)	Denise O'Berry	1/6/2012
9	The Hedgehog Effect: The Secrets of Building High Performance Teams	Manfred F. R. Kets de Vries	1/3/2012
10	We Need To Talk Tough Conversations With Your Employee: From Performance Reviews to Terminations Tackle Any Topic with Sensitivity and Smarts	Lynne Eisaguirre	1/1/2012

Table 31: The latest published books on "Strategy Execution" (8th of February 2012)

Strategy Execution

No.	Title	Author	Published
1	Effective Strategy Execution: Improving Performance with Business Intelligence (Management for Professionals)	Bernd Heesen	1/3/2012
2	Managing Performance in Turbulent Times: Analytics and Insight	Ed Barrows et al	12/6/2011
3	The Living Organization: Transforming Business To Create Extraordinary Results	Norman Wolfe	11/2/2011
4	High Performance Through Process Excellence: From Strategy to Execution with Business Process Management	Mathias Kirchmer	10/14/2011
5	The Enterprise Business Analyst: Developing Creative Solutions to Complex Business Problems	Kathleen B. Hass	9/29/2011
6	Managing the Knowledge-Intensive Firm	NicolajEjler et al	9/29/2011
7	Strategic Planning	Dr. B. Hiriyappa Ph. D.	9/3/2011
8	Management Accounting: Information for Decision-Making and Strategy Execution and myAccountingLab with Pearson eText Student Access Code Card for Management Accounting Package (6th Edition)	Anthony A. Atkinson et al	8/28/2011
9	Corporate Strategy	Dr. B. Hiriyappa Ph. D.	7/6/2011
10	Building High Performance Government Through Lean Six Sigma: A Leader's Guide to Creating Speed, Agility, and Efficiency	Mark Price et al	4/22/2011

Table 32: The latest published books on "Strategic Management" (8th of February 2012)

Strategic Management

No.	Title	Author	Published
1	Plan to Succeed: A Guide to Strategic Planning	Steven C. Stryker	2/16/2012
2	Management Dynamics in Strategic Alliances (Research in Strategic Alliances)	T. K. Das	2/15/2012
3	Good Idea. Now What: How to Move Ideas to Execution	Charles T. Lee	2/14/2012
4	Make Up Your Mind: A Decision Making Guide to Thinking Clearly and Choosing Wisely	Hal Mooz et al	2/14/2012
5	Strategic Management Practices in The Construction Industry: A Dynamic Capabilities View	Muhammad Sapri Pamulu	2/9/2012
6	Strategic Recreation Management	Jay Shivers et al	2/9/2012
7	Strategic Lean Mapping	Steve Borris	2/8/2012
8	Beyond Performance Management: Why, When, and How to Use 40 Tools and Best Practices for Superior Business Performance	Jeremy Hope et al	2/7/2012
9	Collaborate: The Art of We	Dan Sanker	2/7/2012
10	Strategic Management Concepts	Frank T. Rothaermel	2/1/2012

smart**KPIs**.com
The *smart* choice in performance management

TOP KPIS REPORTS

- Extensive collections of the most visited KPIs on smartKPIs.com, across functional areas and industries;
- Thorough analysis of each KPI according to smartKPIs.com documentation forms and standards;
- Proof-of-concept of relevant KPIs, documented at best practice standards.

Reports by Functional Area

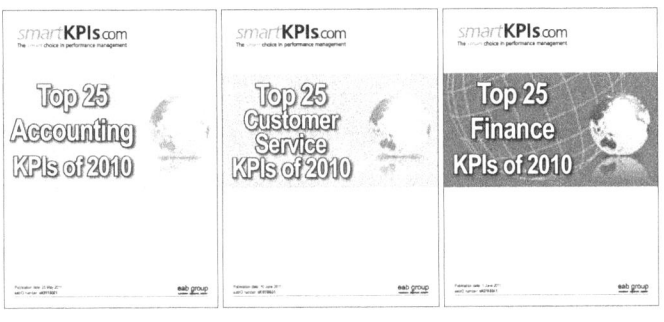

Reports by Industry

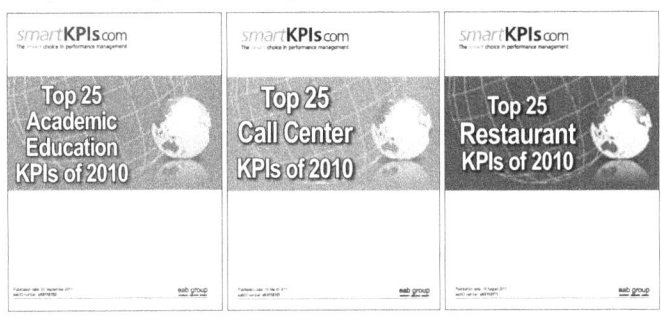

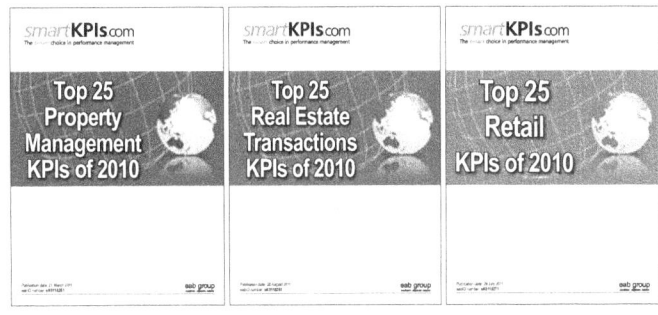

www.smartkpis.com/premium/products/reports/browse-top-kpis-reports

Journal Articles

Academic research is an important enabler for expanding the body of knowledge for Performance Management as a discipline. Table 33 illustrates 15 of the latest articles related to Performance Management. The list was compiled using the search capabilities of The University of Melbourne's library resources and Google scholar search. ▪

Table 33: The Latest Published Peer Reviewed Articles

Rank	Cover	Title	Author	Published
1		Subjective performance appraisal and inequality aversion	Christian Grund	2012
2		Why is Performance Management broken?	Elaine D. Pulakos & Ryan S. O'Leary	2012
3		Performance Management challenges in hybrid NPO/public sector settings - an Irish case	Frank J. Conaty	2012
4		Australian public sector Performance Management: success or stagnation?	Lewis Hawke	2012
5		Developments in public sector performance measurement: a project on producing return on investment metrics for law enforcement	Suresh Cuganesan & David Lacey	2011
6		Linking strategic HRM, Performance Management and organizational effectiveness: perceptions of managers in Singapore	Pauline Stanton & Alan Nankervis	2011
7		The impact of Performance Management on the results of a non-profit organization	André de Waal, Robert Goedegebuure & Patricia Geradts	2011

Rank	Cover	Title	Author	Published
8		Integrating business analytics into strategic planning for better performance	Tobias Klatt, Marten Schlaefke & Klaus Moeller	2011
9		Performance measurement models in facility management: a comparative study	Xianhai Meng & Michael Minogue	2011
10		The use of multiple performance measures and the balanced scorecard (BSC) in Bangladeshi firms: An empirical investigation	MdHabib-Uz-Zaman Khan, Abdel K. Halabi & Kurt Sartorious	2011
11		A 'fruitless obsession with accuracy': The uses of sensemaking in public sector Performance Management	Tom Stannard	2011
12		The organization of discipline: From Performance Management to perversity and punishment	Joe Soss, Richard Fording & Sanford F. Schram	2011
13		Management Innovation and Organizational Performance: The Mediating Effect of Performance Management	Richard M. Walker, Fariborz Damanpour & Carlos A. Devece	2011
14		Improving operational performance by influencing shopfloor behaviour via Performance Management practices	Sander de Leeuw & Jeroen P. Van den Berg	2011
15		Strengthening the link between performance measurement and decision making	Jeannette Taylor	2011

Portals

Online content plays an increasingly influent role in knowledge sharing. Tables 34 and 35 illustrate the Top 10 most visited portals according to the traffic ranking produced by Alexa and Compete. They are two of the best providers of web statistics and their methodologies are fairly well documented. To put traffic statistics into context, worldwide data was analyzed via Alexa and U.S. traffic data was analyzed via Compete. ▪

Table 34: The Most Visited Portals According to Alexa (8th February 2012)

No.	Name	Alexa Traffic Rank
1	www.smartKPIs.com	96841
2	www.KPILibrary.com	112313
3	www.dashboardinsight.com	226794
4	www.b-eye-network.com	308016
5	www.enterprise-dashboard.com	354939
6	www.dashboardspy.com	578136
7	www.dashboardzone.com	633492
8	www.businessintelligence.com	881916
9	www.performanceportal.org	1329870
10	www.performance-measurement.net	4320684

Table 35: The Most Visited Portals According to Compete (13th February 2012)

No.	Name	Compete (U.S. Data Only) Rank
1	www.b-eye-network.com	101466
2	www.KPILibrary.com	271017
3	www.dashboardinsight.com	343170
4	www.enterprise-dashboard.com	726752
5	www.smartKPIs.com	792045
6	www.dashboardspy.com	905020
7	www.dashboardzone.com	1516932
8	www.performance-measurement.net	4345297
9	www.epmreview.com	4531733
10	www.performanceportal.org	N/A

It is clear that the top five most visited portals, are the same whether the data was obtained from Alexa or from Compete. In Alexa's ranking, smartKPIs.com was the most popular website; while in Compete, the figure shows that www.b-eye-network.com had the most traffic. As Alexa provides worldwide data and Compete only gathers information from U.S., this can be interpreted that worldwide, www.smartKPIs.com is the most visited portal, while www.b-eye-network.com is more popular in the US. Overall, it is evident that the themes of Balanced Scorecard, KPI and Business Intelligence generate the most interest. ▪

Communities

There has undoubtedly been an increasing usage of social media. Websites such as LinkedIn, a social network for professionals, provides a platform to share ideas, expertise and best practices within groups, is one such example. LinkedIn was investigated given that it represents the largest community of professionals interested in business topics and has the most active member base in the relevant area. Five types of LinkedIn groups dedicated to Performance Management were identified: Corporate Performance Management (CPM), Balanced Scorecard (BSC), Business Intelligence (BI), Key Performance Indicators (KPIs) and Employee Performance Management (EPM). Each group's member base is represented below. ▪

Table 36: Corporate Performance Management Communities (13th February 2012)

Corporate Performance Management	Members
Corporate Performance Management (CPM)	7036
BI-Business Intelligence & EPM-Enterprise Performance Management Practitioners Group	4211
PMA - Performance Management Association	923

Table 37: Balanced Scorecard Communities (13th February 2012)

Balanced Scorecard	Members
Balanced Scorecard Practitioners Global Network	9815
Balanced Scorecard Group	2351
Balanced Scorecard and Dashboard	2306

Table 38: Business Intelligence Communities (13th February 2012)

Business Intelligence	Members
Business Intelligence Group	7036
Business Intelligence / Data warehouse Leaders	4211
Business Intelligence & Performance Management (BI&CPM)	923

Table 39: Key Performance Indicators Communities (13th February 2012)

Key Performance Indicators	Members
Performance Measurement	2312
Key Performance Indicator (KPI) Users Group	2072
smartKPIs: KPI, Balanced Scorecard, Business Intelligence…	731

Table 40: Employee Performance Management Communities (13th February 2012)

Employee Performance Management	Members
Pay for Performance	1088
Employee Performance Management (HR)	1057
Talent Management Group	933

Software

Performance Management systems require enablers for streamlined operations. Software is a key such enabler, as it supports structuring and processing data. The main research body reviewing software products in Gartner. Three of the Garner research studies are quoted below, reflecting the latest trends in specialized products dedicated to Performance Management. Products were reviewed by organizational level: Corporate Performance Management (supporting organizational strategy implementation), Business Intelligence (supporting operational performance improvements and insight generation) and Employee Performance Management (at individual level). ▨

Corporate Performance Management

The main Garner research paper dedicated to this level is *CPM Suites User Survey 2011*: Customers Rate Their Corporate Performance Management Vendors. In general, organizations implementing Corporate Performance Management (CPM) software appear to be satisfied with its deployment. This is because CPM implementations are considered "relatively low-risk, relatively easy to implement and generate benefits in 12 to 18 months"(Gartner 2011a).

approximately fits a linear regression, suggesting that there is a correlation between Combined Benefits Obtained and Overall Satisfaction.

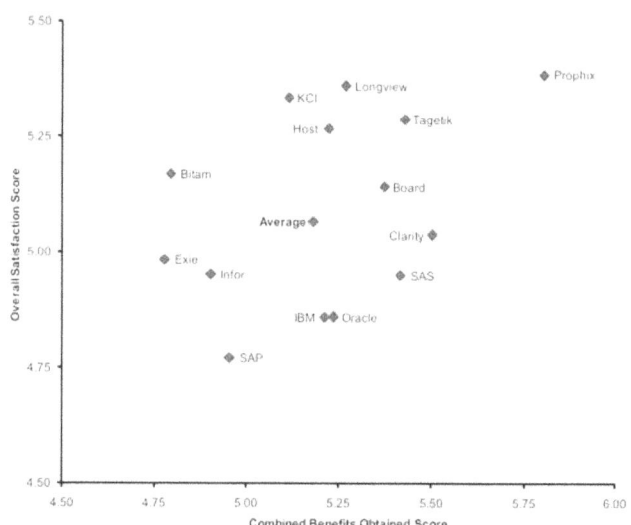

Rating is average of respondents' overall aggregate score by vendor. The chart represents customer perceptions, not Gartner's opinion. The chart may feature vendors that in Gartner's opinion don't deliver the benefits described (N=213).

Figure 31: Combined Benefits Obtained Score vs. Overall Satisfaction Score
Source: Gartner 2011a, CPM Suites User Survey 2011: Customers Rate Their Corporate Performance Management Vendors, by Chandler, N, viewed 13 February 2012, http://my.gartner.com/portal/server.pt?open=512&objID=249&mode=2&PageID=864059&resId=1763015&ref=Browse

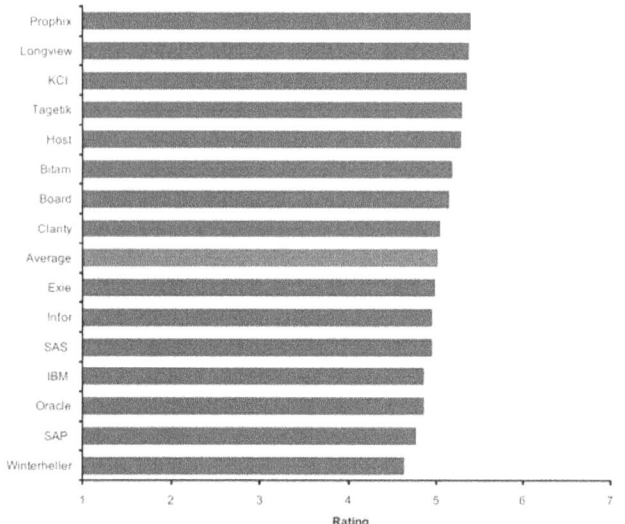

Rating is average of respondents' overall aggregate score by vendor. The chart represents customer perceptions, not Gartner's opinion. The chart may feature vendors that in Gartner's opinion don't deliver the benefits described (N=213).

Figure 30: Corporate Performance Management Software Customer Satisfaction

Overall Satisfaction Versus Business Benefits

Figure 30 shows the distribution of companies when the Combined Benefits Obtained Score is mapped onto the horizontal axis and the Overall Satisfaction Score is mapped onto the vertical axis. The five largest CPM vendors by market share (IBM, SAP, Infor, Oracle and SAS) all perform worse than average in the satisfaction stakes, while most of the niche offerings perform better in the Overall Satisfaction Score. The distribution of companies

Most Common Reasons for Vendor Selection

The most common reasons that organizations put forward when asked why they chose the CPM software vendor are illustrated in Table 40. By looking at the solutions that are being provided by the vendor, as well as the top three reasons why an organization chooses a specific vendor, a new organization wishing to enter the market can focus their marketing approach. ▨

Table 40: The most common reasons for choosing the vendor (Gartner, 2011a)

Vendor	Customer Locations	Top Three Reasons Given for Choosing Vendor
Bitam	Mainly North America and South America, but also worldwide	Functional capabilities, pricing model/TCO, good feedback from references
Board International	Mainly EMEA, but also worldwide	Functional capabilities, expected performance, understanding of business needs
Clarity Systems	Mainly North America, but also worldwide	Expected performance, functional capabilities, quality of RFP response
Exie	Exclusively in EMEA	Implementation methodology, understanding of business needs, functional capabilities
Host Analytics	Mainly North America, but also worldwide	Functional capabilities, pricing model/TCO, expected performance
IBM	Worldwide	Functional capabilities, pricing model/TCO, expected performance
Infor	Worldwide	Functional capabilities, pricing model/TCO, good feedback from references
KCI Computing	Mainly North America, but also worldwide	Functional capabilities, expected performance, vendors expertise
Longview Solutions	Mainly North America, but also worldwide	Functional capabilities, expected performance, vendors expertise
Oracle	Worldwide	Already used other products, functional capabilities, viewed as strategic partner
Prophix Software	Mainly North America, but also worldwide	Functional capabilities, pricing model/TCO, good feedback from references
SAP	Worldwide	Functional capabilities, already used other products, expected performance
SAS	Worldwide	Vendor expertise, already used other products, expected performance
Tagetik	Mainly EMEA, but also worldwide	Understanding of business needs, functional capabilities, pricing model/TCO
Winterheller Software	Mainly EMEA, but also worldwide	Functional capabilities, expected performance, good feedback from references

Business Intelligence

Magic Quadrant For BI 2012

In February each year, Gartner releases one of its most popular research reports: Magic Quadrant for Business Intelligence Platforms.

The latest edition, outlines three main popular areas of interest in the Business Intelligence (BI) Software market:

1. **Integration**, which deals with collaborating data,
2. **Information Delivery**, where reporting is a major aspect and
3. **Analysis**, which involves predictive modelling and processing.

The report reflects that the highest rated vendors are the largest ones, not surprising considering one of the criteria is the ability to execute, which favours size rather than agility. To note is the emergence of vendors new vendors that were not part of the ecosystem just a few years ago. The BI marketplace is evaluated at over $10 billion dollars, attracting new vendors that drive innovation and put pressure on pricing. Overall this is good news for practitioners. ▨

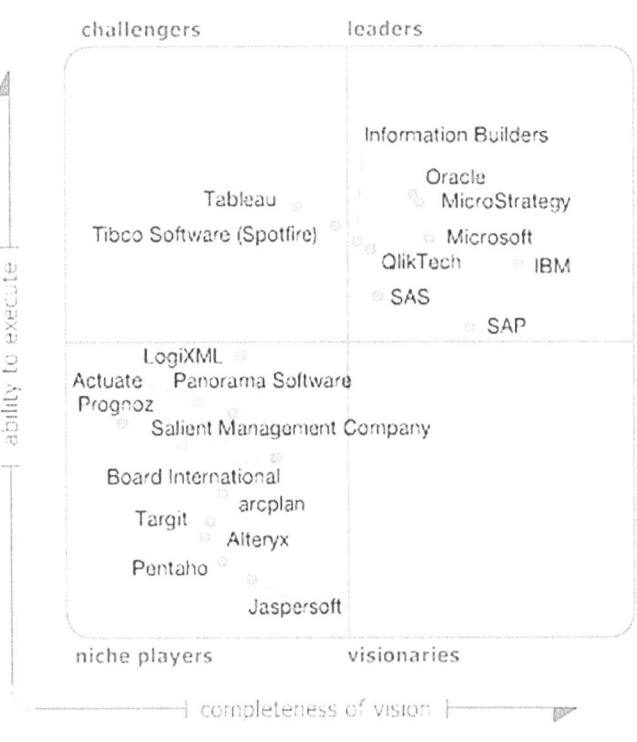

Figure 32: EPM Software Magic Quadrant for 2012
Source: Gartner 2012, Magic Quadrant for Business Intelligence Platforms, Hagerty, S., Richardson, J., Sallam, R.L., viewed 15 February 2012, http://www.gartner.com/DisplayDocument?id=19 15014&ref=g_sitelink&ref=g_SiteLink

Employee Performance Management

Software Magic Quadrant for 2011

Employee Performance Management (EPM) Software is facilitates the automation of performance planning and assessments at individual level. A stronger correlation between effort and outcome and it enables managers to see if there are any employees performing below par and who should be offered further training. As reflected in the Gartner Magic Quadrant for Employee Performance Management Software, EPM Software users identified four main areas of interest and current performance (as of March 2011), listed below:

(on a scale of 1=Not At All Successful to 7=Completely Successful)

- Automation of EPM processes: 5.99/7
- Improve linkage between pay and performance: 5.59/7
- Develop next generation of leaders in the field: 5.41/7
- Improve employee/ associate retention: 5.42/7 ■

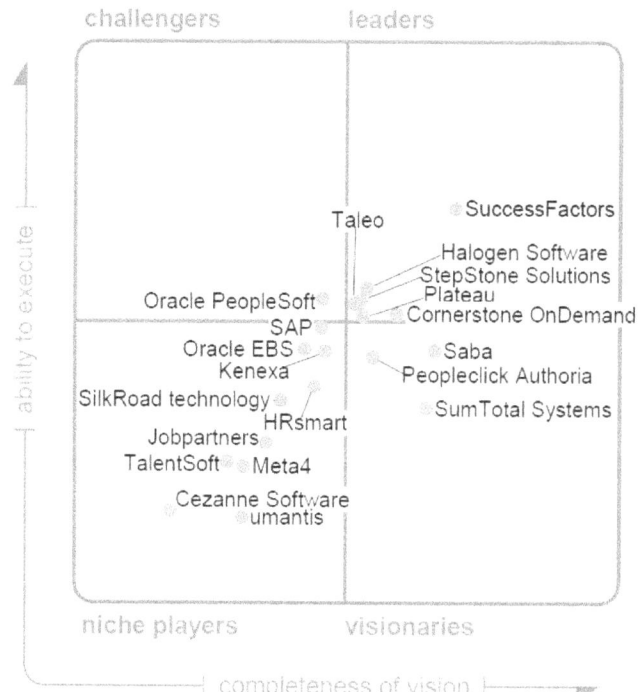

Figure 33: BI Software Magic Quadrant For 2012
Source: Gartner 2011b, Magic Quadrant for Employee Performance Management Software, Gartner, Inc. Freyermuth, J, Holincheck J, Otter, T, viewed 15 Febuary 2012, http://www.gartner.com/id=1606314

INTEGERPERFORM

Business Intelligence Software
Ideal anywhere in the world

TRY THE LIVE DEMO

www.software.integerperform.com
Username: demo
Password: view

TEST

Contact:
info@integerperform.com
for a 30 days trial of the software

BUY

Administrator licence: **$99/month**
Communication (edit) licence: **$30/month**
View only licence: **FREE**

Characteristics

- ✓ Intuitive, robust, fully live and interactive
- ✓ Reliable in any economic environment
- ✓ Offers optimal return on investment

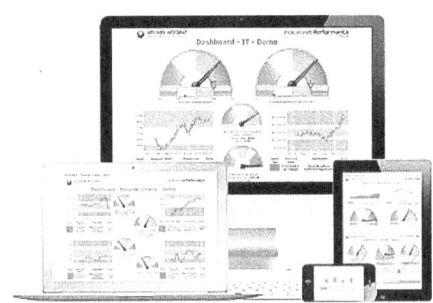

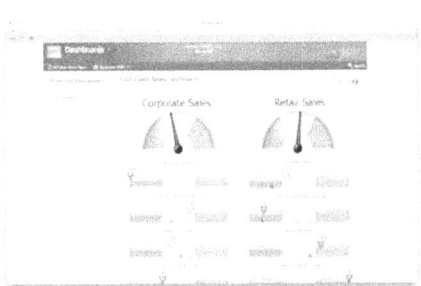

Benefits

- ✓ Real time control of your business
- ✓ Easy monitoring, analysis and reporting of KPis
- ✓ Perfect for Balanced Scorecard automalion
- ✓ Fast consolidalion of information

Configuration

- ✓ Easy to access and to use, fully web-based
- ✓ Possibility of external, in-cloud hosting, as well as on-site
- ✓ Easy to access from any device or location having Internet access

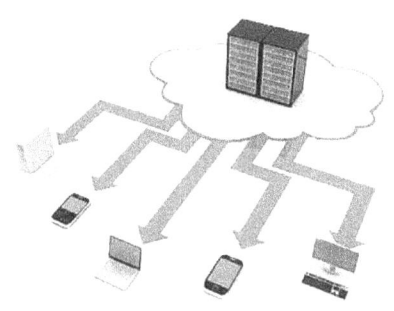

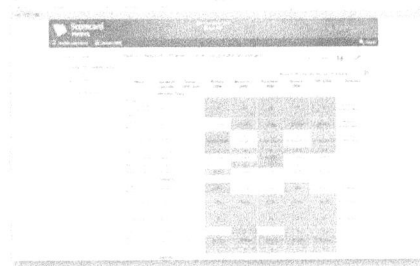

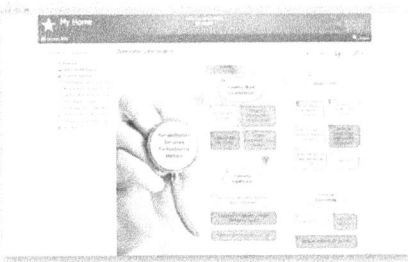

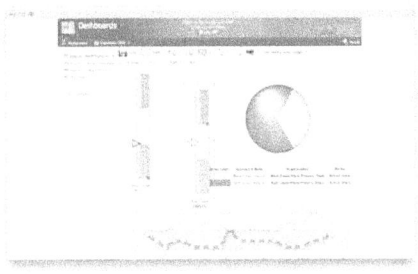

Who uses it?

Cleveland Clinic

U.S.ARMY

FDA

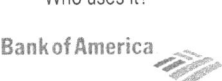
Bank of America

unicef

Walmart

www.integerperform.com/kpi-dashboard-balanced-scorecard-software

The KPI Compendium

The KPI Compendium

20,000+

Key

Performance

Indicators

used in practice

Explore online the most comprehensive catalogue of documented KPI examples.

smart**KPIs**.com

Editorial coordination: Aurel Brudan

THE KPI INSTITUTE

The KPI Institute smart**KPIs**.com

2012 BOOK LAUNCH